PERSONAL FINANCE FOR TEENS 101

THE ULTIMATE GUIDE TO BUDGET, SAVE, INVEST FOR EARLY FINANCIAL INDEPENDENCE

FREDDIE GRANT

CONTENTS

INTRODUCTION

Imagine this: it's a typical Saturday afternoon, and while your friends are out splurging their weekly allowances on the latest video games or trendy clothes, you're at home, scrolling through your budgeting app. You're poring over your expenses lately and analyzing how you can increase your savings over the next year. And you don't necessarily see this as a big sacrifice on your part. You don't think that you're missing out. You know you still have all the opportunities in the world to have fulfilling experiences and spend time with your friends. But you also know that there's a bigger goal at stake here, and it's important that you don't lose sight of the larger picture. This scene might sound familiar, or maybe it's something you aspire to.

Did you know that over half of teenagers like you already have savings (Backman, 2017)? Yes, that's right. Despite the stereotype of teens being impulsive spenders, many are proving this wrong by diligently saving money. And what's even more impressive is that a large portion of these savings isn't just for immediate gratifications like the latest tech gadget or designer sneakers. Instead, teenagers think long-term, saving to fund their college education or for a place they will eventually move into once they leave their parents' homes.

But where does this money come from? On average, teenagers are earning about $465 per month. This income might come from part-time jobs, side hustles, or entrepreneurial ventures. The key takeaway here isn't just the amount but the understanding and value of money that comes with earning it. Each dollar earned is a step toward financial independence and a lesson in financial management.

As a teenager in today's world, you're planning not just for your next purchase but also for your financial future. If you're reading this and thinking, *well, I don't have any savings yet,* or *I'm not really earning my own money,* don't let that dishearten you. The fact that you're holding this book is a sign that you're ready to start. You're here because you want to learn, grow, and, most importantly, take control of your financial future. And that's exactly what we're going to empower you to achieve.

Understandably, you're intimidated by the roadblocks you might be facing. For some of you, it's the anxiety that bubbles up when you think about money and your financial future. This anxiety isn't just a fleeting worry; it's a heavy thought that lingers in the back of your mind. For others, the frustration comes from not knowing how to make your hard-earned money work for you. Maybe you're confused by all the financial jargon, or you feel overwhelmed by the sheer amount of advice out there.

No matter your current situation, whether you're grappling with financial stress or simply seeking ways to optimize your savings, you're not alone in this journey. Every teen faces these challenges at some point. But here's the good news: you're on the brink of something transformative. This book isn't just about teaching you the basics of budgeting or saving. It's about equipping you with the knowledge and tools to turn those challenges into opportunities, to transform your anxiety into confidence, and your frustration into motivation. To do this, we're going to explore the rich and wonderful world of personal finance.

Managing personal finance is not only about money but also understanding how every financial decision you make impacts your life. Each aspect plays a role in your personal finance story, from the cash you earn at your part-time job to the money you save for a concert.

Why should you care about personal finance? Because it's about your future. It's about making sure you're not just surviving but thriving. By mastering personal finance, you equip yourself with the tools to make informed decisions, avoid debt traps, and build a foundation for a secure and fulfilling future.

Personal finance covers a range of areas, and we'll delve into each of these throughout the book:

- Income: Understanding different ways to earn money, be it from jobs, side hustles, or entrepreneurial ventures.
- Spending: Learning to spend wisely, distinguishing needs from wants, and managing expenses.
- Saving: Developing the habit of setting aside money for short-term and long-term goals.
- Investing: Learning how to grow your money through various investment avenues.
- Credit: Learning about credit scores, how to use credit responsibly, and the impact it has on your financial life.

That's just barely scratching the surface of what this book has in store for you! This book is more than just a collection of financial concepts; it's a stepping stone to a more confident and secure financial future. Think of this book as your financial GPS. The world of finance can be complex and intimidating, but you don't have to navigate it through trial and error. We've mapped out the route for you. Each chapter is a step toward understanding how to make smart financial decisions, empowering you to take control of your financial destiny.

Whether you're earning from a part-time job, freelance gigs, or entrepreneurial ventures, this book will teach you how to maximize the potential of every dollar you earn. Even if you're relying on allowance from your parents, you are responsible for overseeing how this money is managed and handled. It's not just about how much you make; it's about how you use what you make. You'll learn strategies for stretching your paycheck further, investing wisely, and laying the groundwork for a financially secure future.

If terms like "investing," "budgeting," and "credit" sound like a foreign language to you right now, don't worry. We're here to translate. This book simplifies the financial maze, breaking down complex concepts into easy-to-understand language and actionable steps. Say goodbye to confusion and hello to clarity. With each page, you'll find yourself more equipped to navigate the world of personal finance with confidence and ease.

Let's be candid: navigating the world of personal finance isn't a walk in the park. It's complex, often confusing, and sometimes feels like a language you haven't learned yet. Everywhere you turn, there are new terms, overwhelming advice, and the nagging worry that a single misstep could lead to financial setbacks. It's a lot to handle, especially at a young age when you're just starting to make decisions that can shape your future.

But here's the good news: it doesn't have to be as hard as it seems. This book is designed to make understanding and managing your finances significantly easier. As you turn these pages, you'll find that what once seemed like a challenging subject becomes approachable and enjoyable. You'll discover that financial terms and concepts are not just for experts but for anyone willing to learn—including you. This book is your toolkit, filled with practical advice, real-life examples, and interactive exercises tailored specifically for teens. It's written with you in mind, addressing your questions, concerns, and aspirations. It's a book that understands where you are now and where you want to be. So, while you can be proud of yourself for picking this book up, there's still a lot of work to do. And this book is going to hold your hand every step of the way.

CHAPTER 1
GET YOUR MONEY-MAKING MIND RIGHT

Wealth is a mindset. It's all about how you think. Money is literally attracted to you or repelled from you.

DAVID SHIRMER

TO BEGIN THIS CHAPTER, let me tell you a story about my nephew Alex. When Alex turned 16, my parents (his grandparents) gave him $100 as a birthday present. Now, Alex had two choices: buy a video game that he had been wanting or save his money toward something else that he could buy in the future. At that time, Alex was saving up for his first car. He had a decision to make. Should he buy the video game and spend the money right away? Should he put the money away until he's ready to buy his first car?

For years, Alex had seen money as something that comes and goes. He would get cash gifts or earn a little from odd jobs, but it never seemed to stick around. Spending gave him immediate satisfaction, a quick hit of happiness, but it was fleeting. This time, however, something felt different. He'd been learning about the power of a savings mindset in school, and something clicked.

Alex realized that each time he spent money without thinking, he gave away a piece of his future freedom. He started to see $100 not just as a means to an immediate end but as a building block toward something bigger. It wasn't just about denying himself the game but empowering his future self.

This simple decision marked the beginning of Alex's journey toward a growth-oriented money mindset. He started to understand that his beliefs about money could either limit or expand his financial potential. By choosing to save, he was taking a small but significant step toward a future where he had more choices, more freedom, and less financial stress.

You see, it didn't matter how much money Alex was getting. He couldn't save a lot of his money growing up because his mindset didn't allow him to. In this chapter, you'll learn all about mindset and how your current beliefs about money might be holding you back. With this chapter, you will not only understand your money mindset but also have the tools to reshape it into one that fosters wealth, not just in your bank account but in your life.

AN INTRODUCTION TO MONEY MINDSET

Money mindset refers to your attitudes, beliefs, and perceptions about money. It's a deeply ingrained set of beliefs that guide how you make, spend, save, and think about money. Your money mindset often reflects a complex mix of past experiences, cultural influences, and the financial habits of those around you.

Why Does Money Mindset Matter?

Many of us grow up with certain beliefs about money that can hold us back. These might include ideas like "money is the root of all evil," "you have to work hard to earn money," or "rich people are greedy." These beliefs are limiting because they create a negative narrative around wealth and success. By recognizing and challenging these beliefs, you can overcome barriers preventing you from achieving financial well-being. Money isn't inherently bad. It's all about how you look at and handle your money that truly matters.

Your mindset plays a crucial role in setting and achieving financial goals. With a positive money mindset, you're more likely to set realistic, achievable goals and take consistent steps toward reaching them. Whether saving for college, starting a business, or buying your first car, a healthy attitude toward money empowers you to plan and persevere. And it isn't just a matter of accumulating wealth for the sake of it. It's about achieving a sense of financial freedom. This means having control over your finances rather than letting them control you. It's about making choices that align with your values and goals, giving you the freedom to live life on your terms.

Developing a healthy money mindset gives you a more positive relationship with money. Instead of viewing money as a source of stress or conflict, you begin to see it as a tool to achieve your dreams and support your values. This shift in perspective can lead to more happiness, less anxiety, and a greater sense of security.

How Do Money Mindsets Develop?

A variety of factors shapes your money mindset:

- **Family and Home Environment:** The way your parents or guardians handle money significantly influences your own beliefs. If money was a source of tension in your household, you might view it as something stressful or negative.
- **Cultural and Societal Influences:** Cultural background and societal norms also play a role. Different cultures have different attitudes toward saving, spending, and wealth, which can shape your views.
- **Personal Experiences:** Your personal experiences with money, such as earning your first paycheck, saving for something you wanted, or facing financial hardship, also contribute to your mindset.
- **Education and Awareness:** The level of financial education you receive, whether at school, at home, or through self-education, impacts your understanding and beliefs about money.

Regardless of what your money mindset is now, remember that it's always a fluid situation. Just because you've been struggling with money in the past doesn't mean that it's always going to be that way. You have the power to change that narrative and make that shift whenever you want.

Do You Have a Positive or Negative Mindset?

Understanding whether you have a positive or negative money mindset is pivotal in shaping your financial future. Let's explore the characteristics of both, which can help you reflect on your current perceptions and attitudes toward money.

Positive Money Mindset

- **Belief in Deserving Wealth:** A positive mindset involves believing that you deserve to be wealthy. This doesn't mean feeling entitled to wealth without effort but rather having the confidence that with hard work and smart decisions, you are worthy of financial success.
- **Taking Responsibility for Financial Well-being:** Those with a positive money mindset take active responsibility for their financial situation. They understand that their choices directly impact their financial health and are proactive in managing their money effectively.
- **Viewing Money as a Tool for Good:** Instead of fearing or idolizing money, a positive mindset sees it as a powerful tool that, when used wisely, can bring about positive change. It's about leveraging financial resources to improve your life and the lives of others.
- **Belief in Abundance:** A key aspect of a positive money mindset is the belief that there is enough wealth to go around. This abundance mindset fosters a sense of optimism and openness to opportunities rather than viewing money as a scarce and competitive resource.
- **Practicing Positive Money Mantras:** Reciting positive affirmations or mantras about money can reinforce a healthy relationship with finances. These mantras might include statements like "I am capable of making smart financial decisions" or "I am on my way to financial freedom."

Negative Money Mindset

- **Chronic Feelings of Scarcity:** If you often feel like you're always broke regardless of your actual financial status, it may indicate a negative mindset. This scarcity mindset can persist even when your bank account says otherwise.

- **Believing Stereotypes about Wealth:** Holding beliefs that rich people are inherently greedy or selfish is a sign of a negative money mindset. This view creates a mental barrier to wealth, associating it with negative traits.
- **Viewing Money as the Root of Evil:** If you think of money as the primary cause of evil or problems in the world, it reflects a negative perception of finances. This belief can hinder your ability to engage with money in a healthy, constructive manner.
- **Guilt Associated with Spending:** Feeling guilty for spending money on yourself, especially for things that bring you joy or improve your life, indicates a negative mindset. It implies a troubled relationship with money, where spending is seen as inherently bad.

Recognizing your money mindset is the first step toward reshaping it. Reflect on these characteristics: do any resonate with you? Understanding whether your mindset leans more toward the positive or negative spectrum is key in beginning the journey toward a healthier financial future. Developing this self-awareness will help you discover what's good and bad about your current mindset and how to strategize moving forward as you shift that perspective into something that favors your goals.

GROWTH VS. FIXED MONEY MINDSETS

In the world of personal finance, mindsets tend to be gauged as being either growth-oriented or fixed.

A growth money mindset is characterized by believing that your financial intelligence and abilities can be developed with time and effort. It's about seeing financial challenges as opportunities for growth, learning from financial mistakes, and understanding that perseverance and smart strategies can improve your financial situation.

For example, Taylor, a high school student, struggles with saving money. However, instead of resigning to this struggle, Taylor decides to learn more about budgeting. She starts tracking expenses and sets small, achievable saving goals, gradually improving her financial habits.

In contrast, a fixed money mindset is the belief that your financial intelligence and abilities are static and cannot change significantly. This mindset often leads to avoiding financial challenges, fearing failure, and feeling helpless in the face of financial difficulties.

Jamie, a high school student, believes he is naturally bad with money. When he receives his allowance or earns money from a part-time job, he spends it quickly, thinking he'll never be good at saving anyway.

This is a very stark difference, for example, but it's worth noting that many people fall along various parts of this spectrum. That means some people toe the very thin line and can lean one way or another. While you might believe that you have a growth mindset, that isn't always necessarily the case. Your habits and tendencies might indicate something different. Here are a few signs that your mindset needs a makeover:

- **Constant Worry About Money:** If you find yourself perpetually worried about money, irrespective of your current financial situation, it's a sign that your mindset may lean toward a fixed perspective.
- **Financial Scarcity Mindset:** Believing that there will never be enough money, regardless of your income or savings, is a hallmark of a fixed mindset. This view can limit your ability to see and seize financial opportunities.
- **Negative Feelings Around Money:** Feelings of guilt, shame, or embarrassment when dealing with money are indicators that your mindset could use a shift. These emotions can stem from past experiences or societal messages about money.
- **Self-Described as 'Bad with Money':** If you often label yourself inherently bad with money, it's a sign that you're operating from a fixed mindset. This belief can prevent you from taking steps to improve your financial skills and knowledge.

Developing a sense of self-awareness and recognizing these signs in yourself is a very important step in moving in the right direction. Now, you are very well aware of all the common attributes of a poor money mindset. Let's discuss what it takes to have that *millionaire mindset* that will allow you to make the most out of your finances. This mindset embodies a series of beliefs and attitudes that many financially successful individuals share. Adopting this mindset can significantly change your approach to personal finance, leading to more effective money management and growth. Here are a few principles of the *millionaire mindset*:

- **Stepping Out of Your Financial Comfort Zone:** The millionaire mindset encourages stepping beyond your financial comfort zone. This means being willing to take calculated risks, whether it's investing in stocks, starting a small business, or simply trying out new ways of saving money. It's about understanding that staying in the safe zone often means missing out on opportunities for financial growth.
- **Changing the Way You Think About Savings:** A key aspect of the millionaire mindset is transforming your approach to savings. It's not just about storing money away; it's about assigning a purpose to each dollar saved. This could mean creating an emergency fund, saving for investment opportunities, or setting aside money for specific future goals. Viewing savings with a sense of purpose turns it into a proactive part of your financial strategy rather than a passive activity.
- **Reconsidering Views on Debt:** In the millionaire mindset, debt is not inherently bad; how you manage it matters. Understanding the difference between 'good debt' and 'bad debt' is critical. Good debt, like a student loan or a mortgage, can be an investment in your future. In contrast, bad debt, like high-interest credit card debt, can hinder financial growth. Reconsidering your views on debt means learning to use it strategically to your advantage.
- **Knowing Where You Stand Financially:** Financial self-awareness is a cornerstone of the millionaire mindset. This involves regularly assessing your financial situation—knowing

your income, understanding your spending habits, tracking your debts, and being aware of your assets. Knowledge is power, and in the realm of personal finance, knowing where you stand is the first step toward making informed decisions.

- **Embracing Learning Opportunities:** A millionaire mindset is characterized by a continuous desire to learn and grow. This includes staying informed about financial matters, seeking advice from financial experts, reading books on personal finance, and even learning from your own financial mistakes. Embrace every opportunity to learn as a stepping stone toward financial mastery.

Adopting a millionaire mindset is about more than just aspiring to be wealthy; it's about cultivating a set of beliefs and habits that can lead to smarter financial decisions and a more secure financial future. It involves a shift in perspective that sees every financial decision as an opportunity to move closer to your goals.

OVERCOME YOUR LIMITING BELIEFS ABOUT MONEY

Limiting beliefs about money are negative assumptions or convictions that hold you back from achieving your financial potential. These beliefs often manifest as internalized narratives that dictate how you interact with and perceive money. They can lead to self-sabotaging financial behaviors and prevent you from realizing your full financial capabilities.

These kinds of beliefs tend to come from a variety of sources, such as:

- **Family Influence:** How your family handles money can significantly impact your beliefs. If you grew up in a household where money was always tight or where wealth was viewed negatively, these experiences could shape your attitudes toward money.
- **Cultural and Societal Norms:** Cultural background and societal messages also play a role. For instance, if society often portrays wealthy people negatively, it might lead to a belief that acquiring wealth is morally questionable.

- **Personal Experiences:** Your own experiences, especially negative ones like financial loss or debt, can foster limiting beliefs about your ability to manage or accumulate wealth.

We've already talked about some of the negative mindsets that certain people might have when it comes to finances, which is closely related to limiting beliefs. Here are a few examples of common limiting beliefs that people might carry:

"I will never be wealthy because I don't come from a rich family."

"Money is the root of all evil."

"Rich people are greedy and selfish."

"I'm just not good with money."

"It's selfish to want a lot of money."

Adopting these kinds of beliefs tends to lead people to develop unhealthy relationships with their finances. These unhealthy relationships can lead to a poor understanding of how money works and how to manage one's money better.

Fortunately, these limiting beliefs are not set in stone. If you have these limiting beliefs, you can work your way out of this kind of mindset by following these tips:

- **Identify and Acknowledge Your Beliefs:** The first step is recognizing your limiting beliefs. Write them down and reflect on how they've influenced your financial decisions.
- **Understand Their Origins:** Analyze where these beliefs come from. Understanding their roots can help you see them for what they are—perceptions, not realities.
- **Challenge and Reframe Your Beliefs:** Challenge each limiting belief's validity. Ask yourself, "Is this belief absolutely true?" and "How does this belief limit me?" Then, reframe it into a more positive and empowering belief. For example, change "I'm not good with money" to "I can learn to manage money effectively."

- **Educate Yourself About Money:** Gain financial knowledge through books, courses, or workshops. Understanding how money works can demystify it and dispel false beliefs.
- **Seek Positive Role Models:** Find people with a healthy relationship with money and learn from them. Seeing others succeed financially can inspire you and demonstrate that your limiting beliefs are not universal truths.
- **Practice Gratitude and Positivity:** Cultivate a habit of being grateful for what you have and optimistic about your financial future. A positive outlook can gradually erode negative beliefs.

DO YOU STRUGGLE WITH MONEY?

To end this chapter, we will help you develop a more profound understanding of your relationship with money. This is important as you try to address and identify limiting beliefs that could potentially be hindering your financial growth. This quiz is designed to help you reflect on your attitudes and behaviors toward money. Answer each question honestly to gain insights into your financial mindset.

What's your first instinct when you receive money (like an allowance or earnings from a job)?

1. Save it
2. Spend it immediately
3. Plan how to use it, balancing saving and spending

How often do you worry about money?

1. Rarely or never
2. Sometimes
3. Frequently or always

What is your reaction to the idea of creating a budget?

1. Positive – it's a useful tool
2. Neutral – it seems helpful but complex

3. Negative – it feels restricting

How do you view wealthy people?

1. As a source of inspiration and learning
2. Indifferently
3. Negatively, as greedy or selfish

Do you believe that you can improve your financial situation through your actions?

1. Yes, definitely
2. Unsure
3. No, it feels beyond my control

When it comes to financial decisions, how confident do you feel?

1. Very confident
2. Somewhat confident
3. Not confident at all

Do you think money management skills can be learned and improved?

1. Yes
2. Maybe, but it's difficult
3. No, you either have it or you don't

How do you react if you have a financial setback (like an unexpected expense)?

1. Calmly find a solution
2. Feel stressed but try to manage
3. Feel overwhelmed and helpless

What do you think about saving money for the future?

1. It's important, and I'm actively doing it
2. It's important, but I struggle with it
3. It doesn't seem necessary or feasible right now

How do you feel after making a significant purchase?

1. Confident, if it was planned and within budget
2. Mixed feelings
3. Guilty or regretful

Scoring:

Mostly 1's: You seem to have a positive and proactive relationship with money. You are likely on the right path toward a healthy financial future.

Mostly 2's: Your relationship with money is a mix of positive and uncertain attitudes. There is room for growth in confidence and financial skills.

Mostly 3's: You may have limiting beliefs and anxieties about money. Focusing on building a healthier financial mindset could be beneficial.

This quiz serves as a starting point for self-reflection. No matter where you are on your financial journey, there is always room for growth and improvement.

As we wrap up our exploration of money mindsets, it's important to reflect on the profound impact your mindset has on your financial journey. The beliefs and attitudes we've discussed in this chapter aren't just abstract concepts; they're the driving forces behind every financial decision you make.

Remember, your relationship with money is dynamic and ever-evolving. It's not set in stone. With each new insight and understanding, you have the power to transform how you interact with and perceive your finances. This transformation is about more than just thinking positively; it's about actively shaping your financial reality through your mindset. In the next chapter, we will explore tangible, real-world strategies for earning money.

CHAPTER 2
GET THAT GUAP

Wealth is not about having a lot of money; it's about having a lot of options.

CHRIS ROCK

"GET THAT GUAP"— a phrase that's all about earning your own money. In this chapter, we shift gears from mindset to motion, from thinking about wealth to actively creating it. Here, you'll discover a plethora of actionable strategies, all tailored to you, the teen ready to take on the world.

Embarking on your journey to earn money isn't just about filling your wallet; it's about exploring opportunities, gaining independence, and understanding the value of hard work and smart decision-making. As a teenager, the ways you can earn money are as diverse as your interests, and this chapter will guide you through various avenues, from traditional part-time jobs to more creative entrepreneurial ventures. The aim is to inspire you to take proactive steps, experiment, and find joy in earning your own money. Whether you're saving for something specific, contributing to family expenses, or just starting to build your financial foundation, these strategies are your stepping stones.

VALUE OF WORK

Even while juggling school and extracurricular activities, teens have numerous opportunities to earn money. Today's world offers a diverse array of avenues for young people to step into the realm of work, be it part-time jobs, internships, freelance gigs, or entrepreneurial ventures. This section is about understanding and embracing the value of work during your teenage years.

Benefits of Working as a Teen

- **Earning Money:** The most immediate benefit of working as a teen is earning your own money. This income can be used for savings, purchases, or even to contribute to household expenses.
- **Building Character:** Working at a young age instills a sense of discipline, dedication, and perseverance. It cultivates a work ethic that will benefit you throughout your life.
- **Skills Development:** The workplace is a classroom in its own right. You'll acquire practical skills—from technical know-how to soft skills like communication and teamwork—that are invaluable for personal and professional growth.
- **Preparation for Adulthood:** Early work experiences prepare you for the realities of adult life, including managing schedules, meeting responsibilities, and navigating workplace dynamics.
- **Hands-On Financial Management:** Earning money teaches you about budgeting, saving, and spending wisely. It offers hands-on experience in managing finances, an essential skill for adult life.
- **Sense of Responsibility:** Balancing work with other commitments nurtures a sense of responsibility and time management, traits that are highly beneficial in both personal and professional realms.

Cons of Working as a Teen

- **Pressure on Childhood:** Some argue that working at a young age might push teens to grow up too fast, missing out on some aspects of their childhood.
- **Impact on Schoolwork:** Balancing work and school can be challenging. There's a risk that employment might detract from the time and energy needed for academic pursuits.
- **Potential for Misuse of Income:** There's also a concern that the money earned might be spent on unproductive or harmful activities. Without proper guidance and self-control, financial freedom can lead to undesirable habits.

While acknowledging the potential cons associated with working as a teen, it's important to recognize that these challenges can be effectively managed. The right approach minimizes the drawbacks, ensuring that the work experience is enriching and balanced.

First off, maintaining a healthy balance between work and leisure is key. It's also important for you to set aside time for hobbies, relaxation, and socializing to enjoy your teenage years fully. Additionally, academics should remain a top priority. By managing time efficiently and possibly choosing flexible work options, you can ensure that your job does not negatively impact your school performance.

The benefits of working during your teenage years far surpass the potential drawbacks. The practical experience, financial literacy, work ethic, and life skills gained from early work experiences are invaluable assets that lay the foundation for future success. These benefits extend far beyond immediate financial gain; they contribute to character building, instill a sense of independence, and provide a head start in understanding the complexities of the adult financial world.

WAYS TO MAKE MONEY

Passive Income

As we delve into the various ways teens can earn money, it's important to start with an intriguing and immensely valuable concept: passive income. Passive income is essentially money you earn in a way that requires little to no daily effort to maintain. It's all about putting your money to work for you instead of you working for your money.

Passive income is particularly ideal for teens, as it aligns perfectly with the need to balance earnings with school responsibilities. The beauty of passive income lies in its ability to generate earnings without taking away significant time from your studies, extracurricular activities, or social life. While it might require some initial effort or investment, the ongoing time commitment is usually minimal.

Now, let's explore various methods to earn money, both active and passive. The goal is to provide you with a range of options so you can find what best suits your interests, skills, and schedule. Remember, the journey to financial success isn't just about how much you make but how smartly you make it work for you.

- **Stock Market Investment:** Investing in the stock market involves buying shares of companies. The idea is to purchase these shares at a lower price and potentially sell them at a higher price or earn dividends if the company distributes profits. This can be a way for teens to start learning about investing, though it requires research and understanding of the market risks. We will explore stock market investments more thoroughly in a later chapter.
- **Content Creation:** Content creation involves producing and sharing media like blog posts, videos, or photos online. Content creators can earn money through ad revenue, sponsorships, or selling digital products. The key is to create engaging content that attracts a sizable audience.
- **Digital Products:** Digital products can include ebooks, courses, graphic designs, and software. Once created, these products can be sold repeatedly without needing physical inventory, offering a potential source of ongoing income. Teens with a knack for writing, design, or coding can particularly benefit from this.
- **Affiliate Marketing:** Affiliate marketing involves promoting products or services and earning a commission for each sale or referral. This can be done through a blog, social media, or a YouTube channel. It requires building an audience and choosing products that align with your interests and your audience's preferences.

- **Podcasting:** Starting a podcast can also generate income, primarily through sponsorships, advertisements, and listener donations. While it requires initial effort in content creation and building an audience, a successful podcast can become a steady source of income.
- **YouTube Channel:** Creating a YouTube channel and generating revenue through ads, sponsorships, and merchandise sales is another way to earn passively. Like podcasting, it requires consistent content creation and audience engagement, but once established, it can provide ongoing income.

Each of these passive income streams has its own set of challenges and learning curves, but they all offer the opportunity to earn money without the ongoing time commitment of a traditional job.

Summer or Part-Time Jobs

In contrast to passive income sources, actively working in the summer or part-time jobs is a more traditional way for teens to earn money. These jobs not only provide a steady income but also offer valuable work experience. Choosing a job you think you could do well in is very important. Take a look at what skills you have or want to develop, and pursue a job that aligns with those skills:

- **Sales or Retail:** Working in retail involves assisting customers, managing inventory, and handling transactions. The average pay is around $10-$15 per hour, varying by location and store.
- **Babysitting:** Babysitters care for children, ensuring their safety and managing activities or meals. Typically, babysitters can earn $10-$20 per hour, depending on location and number of children.
- **Lawn Care or Gardening Services:** This job includes mowing lawns, planting, weeding, and general garden maintenance. Based on the services offered, expect to earn around $10-$20 per hour.
- **Tutoring:** Tutors help other students understand academic subjects. This job requires a good understanding of the subject

matter. Depending on the subject and location, tutors can earn between $15-$30 per hour.

- **Food and Beverage Services:** Roles in food service include working as a server, dishwasher, or restaurant host. Pay typically ranges from $9-$15 per hour, excluding potential tips for servers.
- **Dog Walking/Pet Sitting:** This job involves walking dogs and caring for pets while owners are away. Dog walkers and pet sitters can earn around $10-$20 per walk or sitting.

These jobs not only provide immediate income but also help develop essential skills like time management, customer service, and responsibility. The pay rates are average estimates and can vary based on location, experience, and the employer.

BALANCING SCHOOL AND PART-TIME WORK

Juggling school responsibilities with a part-time job can be challenging, but with proper planning and organization, it's definitely achievable. Maintaining a balance between work and school is extremely important, as it ensures you don't compromise your education while gaining valuable work experience. Let's explore how to manage this balance effectively.

Structure Your Work

Organizing your work commitments in a structured manner is key. This means being clear about your work hours and what's expected of you in your job. Communicate with your employer about school commitments; most will accommodate your academic schedule. Consider seasonal work during school breaks or a job with flexible hours during the school year.

Find a Work Schedule That Aligns With Your School Schedule

Choose a job with hours that complement your school schedule. This might mean working after school, on weekends, or during school holidays. Avoid over-scheduling yourself on school days, as this can lead to burnout and negatively impact your academic performance.

Always Prioritize Academics

Remember that your primary focus at this stage of your life should be your education. Work should not interfere with your school responsibilities. If you find your job is affecting your schoolwork, it's time to reassess your work commitments. Openly communicate with your employer about reducing hours if necessary.

Create a Homework Plan

Develop a realistic plan for completing homework and studying. This might involve setting aside specific hours each day for schoolwork, using study halls effectively, or dedicating weekends to catch up on assignments. Staying organized with a planner or digital calendar can help you keep track of both school deadlines and work shifts.

Reduce Distractions

When balancing work and school, it's crucial to make the most of your time. This means minimizing distractions during both study and work hours. Create a dedicated study space free from interruptions, and be mindful of how you spend your time on social media or other non-essential activities.

MEETING THE TAX MAN

Understanding taxes can be incredibly intimidating, especially if you're a teenager looking to enter the workforce for the first time. However, as daunting as it might be, taxes are important aspects of financial literacy. And don't worry. It's not as complicated as you might think. In this section, we'll break down the concept of taxes in as simple and uncomplicated a manner as possible.

Why Pay Taxes Anyway?

Taxes are essential for funding public services and infrastructure, like roads, schools, healthcare, and Social Security. By paying taxes, you contribute to the development and maintenance of these essential services, playing a part in the betterment of society. It's all a part of being a responsible member of your community.

What are Income Taxes, and Should You Worry About Them as a Teen?

Income tax is a tax levied by governments on the income earned by individuals and businesses. As a teen, if you have a job, you're likely to encounter income taxes. However, whether you need to worry about them depends on how much you earn. There are specific income thresholds that determine if you need to file a tax return.

Tax Brackets and Federal Income Tax Rates

Tax brackets are ranges of income taxed at specific rates. The United States uses a progressive tax system, meaning the more money you earn, the higher the percentage of tax you pay on your top dollar. These brackets and rates can change, so staying updated or consulting a tax professional is important.

Net vs. Gross Income

If you officially become a member of the workforce, the number one thing that you might be looking forward to is your paycheck. Of course! Any kid would be thrilled at the prospect of being compensated for their work. However, it's important that you understand two key terms that are associated with your salary: Gross and Net.

- **Gross Income:** is the total amount you earn before any taxes or deductions are taken out.
- **Net Income:** is what you take home after taxes and other deductions are subtracted from your gross income.

So, just because you might earn a gross salary of a certain amount doesn't necessarily mean that you can take all of that money home. Depending on how much money you earn and what kind of employment benefits you are getting from your work, your net income is what determines how much money you get to keep after taxes and other deductions.

Who is Required to File and Pay Taxes?

Generally, if you're a teen with a job, you may need to file a tax return if your earned income exceeds certain thresholds. This also depends on whether you're considered a dependent on someone else's tax return, usually your parents. The specific thresholds can vary each year, so checking the current requirements is essential. Currently, any income earned as a result of direct salaries, wages, or fees that amounts to more than $12,950 in a year is taxable. Additionally, any income that comes as a result of capital gains, royalties, or dividends exceeding the amount of $1,150 annually is also taxable. But again, these figures can change, so it's best to do your own research to keep yourself updated.

How to File Your Income Tax Return

If you find that your income certainly *is* taxable, you will have to file your income tax returns. Don't worry. The process is relatively straight-forward. Just follow these steps:

1. **Gather Documents:** Collect all necessary documents, including W-2 forms from employers and any other income statements.
2. **Choose Your Filing Status:** Most teens will file as single. If you're a dependent, this will impact your tax return.
3. **Fill Out the Tax Return:** You can fill out your tax return using IRS Form 1040. There are also various software and online services that can guide you through the process.
4. **Submit Your Return:** You can file your return electronically or mail it to the IRS. Make sure to do this by the deadline (usually April 15).
5. **Keep Records:** Keep copies of your return and all documents for at least three years after filing.

GET ON THE JOB-HUNT!

To end this chapter, it's time to put your learning into action. This interactive exercise is designed to help you transition from theory to practice.

Journaling Session

Take a moment to reflect on all the income-generating ideas we've discussed—both passive income opportunities and part-time or summer jobs. Now, in your journal, list five jobs or income ideas that resonate with you and seem appealing. These could be jobs you feel passionate about, gigs that align with your skills, or passive income ventures that intrigue you.

For each job or idea, write a brief reason why it interests you. This could be related to your hobbies, your future career goals, or simply a desire to learn a new skill. Here's an example:

1. **Tutoring in Mathematics:** I'm good at math and enjoy helping others understand it.
2. **Creating and Selling Digital Art:** I love drawing and want to explore how I can earn from my hobby.
3. **... etc.**

Research is key. Look into what steps you need to take to get started, whether it's getting a certification, setting up an online shop, or creating a portfolio of your work. Set small, achievable goals for each idea to begin your journey toward earning money.

Create Accounts on Job Search Sites

A practical step to finding part-time or summer jobs is to create accounts on job search websites like Indeed or ZipRecruiter. These platforms offer a wide range of job listings and can be a valuable resource in your job hunt:

- Start by setting up your profile. Include any relevant experience, skills, and your educational background.
- Use filters to search for jobs that suit your interests, skills, and availability.
- Regularly check for new postings and apply to the positions that interest you.

Remember, the purpose of this exercise is to encourage you to take the first steps toward earning your own money. It's about taking initiative and being proactive in your financial journey. In the next chapter, expect to be exposed to the idea of turning your creative ideas, passions, and skills into viable business ventures that will give you a sustainable income.

CHAPTER 3
TURN IDEAS INTO ENTERPRISES

If you push through that feeling of being scared, that feeling of taking a risk, really amazing things can happen.

MARISSA MAYER

BEFORE WE GET into the meat of this chapter, I want to talk about the young life of an incredible woman named Maya Penn, a remarkable teen entrepreneur who started her journey at just eight years old. Maya's story began with her passion for art and design. She decided to turn her love for drawing into a business; thus, her company, Maya's Ideas, was born. Maya started creating eco-friendly clothing and accessories and selling them online. But her ambitions didn't stop there. She did all of these before she even turned 10!

As her business grew, Maya expanded her vision. She began using her platform to advocate for environmental causes and women's rights. By the time she was a teenager, Maya had not only built a successful online store but also became a noted philanthropist and activist. Her dedication and entrepreneurial spirit led her to give TED talks and even catch the attention of major media outlets.

Now, Maya is 23 years old and can call herself an award-winning CEO, eco-designer, and a source of inspiration for many young entrepreneurs around the world. Her success story demonstrates that with passion, determination, and a willingness to learn, young entrepreneurs can make a significant impact.

WHY ENTREPRENEURSHIP?

When you think about getting a job and earning an income, you might envision someone who clocks into their office in the morning and then clocks out late in the afternoon. They go home, do whatever they want to do, and then return to the office the next day to repeat the process. And for many people, this is what life looks like on a daily basis. In truth, 9-5 jobs are often seen as the safe choice. You get a steady paycheck, some benefits, and, if you're lucky, a cool work environment. But here's the thing: no matter how hard you work in a typical job, your paycheck is pretty much set. Sure, you might get a raise now and then, but there's a limit to how much you can earn.

There's also that uncertainty that comes with job insecurity. Even if you're doing great, if the company isn't doing well, your job could be on the line. That's not in your control. On top of that, you won't have much control over your time either. In most traditional jobs, you can't just decide to take a day off whenever you want, and your daily tasks are usually decided by someone else.

Now, when you're still in school, this is an even bigger problem. You will find it nearly impossible to establish a 9-5 job because of your academic duties. Fitting a strict job schedule around your classes and homework can be really challenging.

Benefits of Being a Teenpreneur

Embracing entrepreneurship as a teenager, or becoming a *teenpreneur*, isn't just about having opportunities that transcend a traditional 9-5 framework. It's a venture that offers a multitude of benefits. These advantages extend far beyond the immediate financial gains and set the foundation for personal and professional growth. Let's delve into these benefits in detail:

- **Development of Life Skills:** Running your own business means constantly facing new challenges. This fosters essential problem-solving and critical-thinking skills as you navigate various obstacles and make strategic decisions. Being an entrepreneur also teaches you to bounce back from setbacks and adapt to changing circumstances.

- **Improved Time Management:** Juggling schoolwork with business responsibilities requires effective time management. As a teenpreneur, you'll quickly learn how to prioritize tasks and manage your time efficiently.
- **Enhanced Financial Skills:** Running a business involves managing finances, which means you'll get hands-on experience in budgeting, forecasting, and financial planning. These skills are critical for personal financial success as well.
- **More Secure Future:** Starting a business as a teen gives you a head start in your career. The experience and skills gained can pave the way for future job opportunities or entrepreneurial ventures. Also, the income from your business can contribute to savings, investments, and financial security in the long run.
- **Freedom and Flexibility:** As a teenpreneur, you have the flexibility to set your own hours and work environment. This freedom allows you to work in a way that best suits your lifestyle and preferences, especially if you have academic duties that require your attention.
- **Expanded Social Support Base:** Entrepreneurship opens doors to meeting new people, from customers to other business owners. This network can provide support, advice, and opportunities for collaboration. Running a business can also increase your involvement in the community, whether through local events, charities, or collaborations.
- **Access to Mentorship:** Many experienced business owners are eager to mentor young entrepreneurs. This mentorship can provide invaluable guidance, support, and learning opportunities.
- **More Energy and Passion in Youth:** As a teenager, you bring energy and a fresh perspective to the business world. This enthusiasm can be a driving force in the success of your business. Also, if you're passionate about something, you're more likely to enjoy what you're doing and stay motivated.

In truth, entrepreneurship isn't necessarily for everyone, and that's okay. However, the skills and experiences gained through teen entrepreneurship are not just about building a business; they're about building yourself. So, if you feel like this is a vocation that's worth exploring, go ahead and do so while you're young!

DOES PASSION MATTER?

Passion isn't strictly a *necessity* when it comes to starting a business. But many will argue that you would never be able to scale and grow your business if you aren't passionate about it. You wouldn't be able to exert the same kind of effort and energy toward something you're not passionate about. Passion is the spark that ignites the flame of innovation. When you're passionate about your business idea, it shows in the creativity and originality of your approach. This enthusiasm often leads to unique solutions and breakthroughs that might not be possible without a deep, personal interest in the subject.

The road of entrepreneurship is filled with highs and lows. Passion serves as the fuel that keeps you moving forward, even during challenging times. It's the energy that powers long nights of work and drives you to go the extra mile. Motivation is something that many people struggle with. But when you're passionate about something, you don't need to manufacture motivation out of thin air to work on it. Your passion gives you enough fuel to stay determined even when you're faced with adversity. Starting a business, especially as a teenager, can be daunting. Passion helps to overshadow fear, giving you the courage to take risks and step out of your comfort zone. When you are passionate about your venture, the excitement often outweighs the fear of failure.

Investors aren't just interested in the idea; they're interested in the entrepreneur behind it. A passionate entrepreneur is often more convincing and inspiring. This passion can be infectious, making your venture more attractive to potential investors, as it demonstrates commitment and belief in your business.

How to Discover Your Passion

Now, we've discussed how essential passion is for any budding entrepreneur. But how exactly do you go about discovering what your passion is? After all, not everyone is privileged enough to be able to discover what they're passionate about at an early age. If you haven't found what you're passionate about yet, that's okay. You're still young, and you have time. But that doesn't mean that you should just be waiting idly by. Here are a few things that you can do as you try to figure out what you can truly be passionate about:

- **List Your Interests:** Start by making a list of activities that you enjoy or topics that you find intriguing. Think about what excites you, what you can spend hours doing without feeling bored, or what you often read about or discuss with enthusiasm.
- **Recall Your Favorite Experiences:** Think back to moments when you felt most alive or fulfilled. What were you doing? These memories can offer clues about your passions.
- **Try New Things:** Sometimes, you discover your passion by stepping out of your comfort zone. Try different activities, join clubs, or attend workshops. Exploration is key to uncovering hidden interests.
- **Volunteer or Shadow:** Volunteering in various fields or shadowing professionals can provide insight into what you enjoy and where your interests lie.
- **Notice What Absorbs You:** What are the topics or activities that you can get lost in for hours? These are often indicators of your true passions.
- **Observe Your Curiosity:** Notice the topics or ideas that make you curious and eager to explore more. Your natural curiosity can lead you to your passion.
- **Ask for Insights:** Sometimes, friends and family can offer valuable perspectives. They might notice a passion in you that you haven't recognized yourself.
- **Identify Patterns:** Look for recurring themes in your interests and activities. Do you always gravitate towards certain topics or types of tasks?

Remember, discovering your passion is a personal journey and can take time. It's about exploration, self-reflection, and being open to new experiences. Once you identify what truly excites and motivates you, you can start to envision a business idea that aligns with this passion, setting the stage for a fulfilling and successful entrepreneurial venture.

STARTING A BUSINESS

Embarking on an entrepreneurial journey is always an exciting process. But given that you're still young, you might not have any idea how or where to start. That's fine. Everyone who has ever made something of themselves started out with not knowing what to do. Let's take some time to reflect on the foundational aspects of launching your enterprise and polish your business ideas.

What to Consider When Thinking of Business Ideas

Convenience and Accessibility

A home-based business or one that's located nearby is ideal for teens. This setup reduces travel time and costs and ensures you can manage the business in a safe, familiar environment. Examples include online businesses, tutoring services provided at home, or a neighborhood lawn care service. Utilize the resources you already have at home, like a computer for a web design business or a kitchen for a baking venture. This approach saves money and makes juggling business with schoolwork easier.

Financial Investment

Look for business ideas that require minimal start-up costs. This could mean offering a service that relies on your skills (like graphic design, tutoring, or social media management) rather than selling physical products, which require upfront investment for inventory. You can also leverage free online tools and platforms for marketing, communication, and management. For example, use social media for promotion, free software for designing, or platforms like Etsy or eBay for selling.

Flexible Hours

A business idea should allow you to work flexible hours that don't interfere with your school and extracurricular activities. For instance, a freelance writing business or creating digital art can be done anytime that suits you.

Also, consider business ideas that can be ramped up or down based on your availability. Seasonal businesses (like holiday decorating/event organizing) or project-based work (like event photography) can be great options.

How to Decide Which Businesses to Start

We've already reviewed a list of potential business ideas, like tutoring, photography, dog-walking, or babysitting. Now, it's time to hone in on which one is right for you. Making this decision involves several key factors that align with your personal circumstances, goals, and resources. Let's break down these considerations:

Consider Your Lifestyle

Think about how a business fits into your daily life. If you're an early riser, a morning paper route or breakfast delivery service could work. If you're a night owl, consider tasks you can do in the evening, like online tutoring. It's important to choose a business that aligns with your interests and hobbies. A landscaping or dog-walking business might be ideal if you love being outdoors.

Compare Your Options

For each business idea, list the pros and cons. Consider factors like required time, potential income, and personal enjoyment. Talk to friends, family, or mentors about your ideas. They can offer insights and perspectives you might not have considered.

Determine Your Budget

Calculate the initial investment needed for each business idea. Some, like digital content creation, might require minimal investment, while others, like photography, might require equipment. Aside from that, consider the ongoing costs of running the business, such as supplies, transportation, or website maintenance.

Start Small

Consider starting on a small scale to test the viability of your business. For example, begin tutoring one or two students before expanding.

Starting small reduces financial risk and allows you to learn and adjust as you grow your business.

Find Your Specialization

Within your chosen field, find a specific niche or specialization that sets you apart. For example, specialize in math tutoring or pet photography. This will help you market yourself with an actual identity that customers will find reassuring. Choose a specialization that is in demand in your area or among your target audience.

Do Your Research

Do all the research beforehand. For example, identify where you can source the necessary goods or services if necessary. Look for quality and affordability. Consider networking opportunities to find suppliers, collaborators, or partners. Really think about how you can start your business off on the right foot.

Look at the Competition

Research who else is offering similar products or services in your area. What can you offer that's different or better? Analyze what successful competitors are doing well and where there might be gaps in the market.

STEPS FOR STARTING A BUSINESS AS A TEEN

Starting a business as a teen is an exciting endeavor, but it's not something you should rush into without a plan. There's a method to the entrepreneurial madness. Doing things the right way from the start can help you minimize major obstacles or setbacks later on. Here are the major steps of launching a business the right way:

Research Potential Business Ideas

When researching potential business ideas, consider the following:

- **Target Market:** Understand who your potential customers are. What are their needs, preferences, and buying behaviors? Your target market will influence many of your business decisions.

- **Unique Selling Point (USP):** Determine what differentiates your business from others. Your USP is what will attract customers to your product or service instead of a competitor's.
- **Client Needs:** Conduct surveys, interviews, or research to understand what your potential clients want. This will help in tailoring your products or services to meet their needs.

Find a Mentor or Business Coach

Seek out someone with business experience to mentor or coach you. They can provide valuable advice, help you navigate challenges, and offer insights from their own experiences.

Develop a Business Plan

A business plan is important as it helps establish the foundation and direction for your business moving forward. There are many ways to create a business plan, but it should typically include a few key details such as services or products offered, target clients, financial forecasts, and more. We'll work on a business plan template together at the end of this chapter to help you get started.

Choose Your Business Structure

There are various ways you can choose to set up your business:

- **Sole Proprietorship:** A simple structure where you own the business entirely.
- **Partnership:** This might be a suitable structure for starting a business with someone else.
- **Limited Liability Company (LLC):** Offers protection for your personal assets and has tax benefits but is more complex to set up.

Understand Rules, Regulations, and Taxes

If you're looking to legitimize your business, you need to know how to follow all the rules and regulations that come with being a business owner. Take these details into consideration:

- **Legalities for Teen Entrepreneurs:** Research the legal requirements for starting a business as a minor in your area.
- **Parental or Guardian Involvement:** Determine if you need an adult to legally set up the business structure or bank accounts.
- **State Regulations:** Look into any specific regulations or licenses required in your state.
- **Taxes:** Understand the tax implications of your business structure and earnings.

Secure Your Financing

If necessary, you will need to fund your business at the start to secure assets, merchandise, or equipment that you need to get your business off the ground. If you have money saved up, you can always use that. But you can always go different routes, such as asking for investments from your family and loved ones. You can even look into applying for loans or grants.

BUSINESS PLAN TEMPLATE

As we established, creating a business plan is a pivotal step in starting your entrepreneurial journey. This template will guide you through the key components of a business plan. Use this as a starting point to map out your business idea and strategies. Feel free to adjust it according to your specific needs and goals.

1. Executive Summary

- **Business Name:** [Your Business Name]
- **Mission Statement:** A brief statement about what your business aims to achieve.
- **Business Goals:** Short-term and long-term goals for your business.

2. Business Description

- **Business Concept:** Describe your business idea in detail.
- **Unique Selling Proposition (USP):** What distinguishes your business from competitors?

- **Target Market:** Who are your customers?
- **Location:** Where will your business operate?

3. Market Analysis

- **Industry Overview:** A brief overview of the industry you're entering.
- **Target Market Analysis:** Characteristics, size, and potential growth of your target market.
- **Competition Analysis:** Identify your main competitors and analyze their strengths and weaknesses.

4. Marketing and Sales Strategy

- **Marketing Strategy:** How will you attract and retain customers? Include online and offline marketing tactics.
- **Sales Strategy:** How will you sell your product or service? Think about pricing, sales channels, and sales tactics.

5. Operations Plan

- **Production:** How and where will your product or service be produced?
- **Suppliers:** Who will supply the materials or products needed?
- **Facilities:** Describe the physical space needed for your business.
- **Technology:** What technology or software is required for your operations?

6. Organizational Structure

- **Management Team:** If applicable, list the key members of your business team and their roles.
- **Legal Structure:** Will your business be a sole proprietorship, partnership, or LLC?
- **Personnel Plan:** Do you plan to hire employees? If so, what roles will they play?

7. Financial Plan

- **Start-up Costs:** An estimate of the initial costs to start your business.
- **Revenue Projections:** Forecast your revenue (the amount of money you make) for the first year.
- **Operating Expenses:** Monthly or annual estimates of ongoing operational costs.
- **Break-Even Analysis:** Calculate when your business will start to make a profit.

8. Appendices

Attach any additional documents that support your business plan, such as market research data, examples of promotional material, or resumes of key personnel.

Great work so far! We're still very early in this journey, but you've already grown and amassed so much knowledge about how you can take better control of your finances and life. In the next chapter, we're going to double down on our momentum and dive deeper into the world of banking.

CHAPTER 4
THE BUILDING BLOCKS OF BANKING

Money looks better in the bank than on your feet.

SOPHIA AMORUSO

IMAGINE A WORLD WITHOUT BANKS! Well, actually, since you're a teen, there's a good chance that you've never had to transact with any kind of bank before. After all, banking is an activity that's reserved for adults, right? Not necessarily. Banking might seem complex or even intimidating at first glance, but it's a key aspect of managing your money effectively. Whether you're saving for college, managing earnings from your entrepreneurial ventures, or simply planning for the future, understanding how banks work is fundamental.

BANKING 101

A bank is a financial institution licensed to receive deposits and make loans. It serves as a safe place to store money, but it does much more than just keep it under lock and key. Banks offer various products and services like saving accounts, checking accounts, loans, credit cards, and more.

Think of a bank as a safe house for your money. Instead of keeping all your cash under your mattress (which is risky!), you deposit it in a bank. This is not just safer; it also makes managing your money easier. When you store your money in a savings account, the bank pays you interest. This is a bit like earning a small rent on your money for letting the bank hold onto it. The bank uses your money to give out loans to others, and in return for using your money, they pay you interest.

Just like you can store and grow your money in a bank, you can also borrow it. For example, people take bank loans to buy houses and cars or even start a business. The bank charges them interest for borrowing that money, which is how banks make a profit. Banks also offer services like helping you manage your money, issuing credit and debit cards, and providing online banking services that let you handle your finances from your phone or computer.

Again, there's this notion that banks only serve adults and working professionals exclusively. But that isn't true. Many commercial banks these days are offering financial products and services that are specifically designed for younger people. So, while you might think that your trusty little piggy bank will do for now, think again. There are so many benefits to availing the services of a bank, such as:

- Your money is always kept safe.
- Transacting with family and friends (especially digitally) becomes a lot simpler.
- You can pay your bills more easily.
- You can set up alerts for savings or for paying bills.
- You gain access to other products or services that the bank is offering.
- You have the ability to make online transactions for purchases.
- It will be easier for you to manage your money.

Choosing the Right Bank for Your Needs

Selecting the right bank is like choosing a good friend to trust with your money. It's an important decision, as the right bank can support your financial growth and make managing your money easier. Sure, you always have the option to switch banks down the line if you find that it's just not a good fit. But you want to avoid the hassle of doing so as much as possible. With that, it's important that you think deeply about what kind of factors you need to consider when choosing a bank that meets your specific needs and goals.

Choosing the Right Account

Different banks offer various types of accounts. As a teen, you might be interested in checking accounts for everyday transactions or savings accounts for stashing away money for future goals. Decide what type of account suits your needs the best. Some banks offer accounts specifically for teenagers, which might come with parental oversight options and educational resources. Go over your options together with your parents or guardians and see what best suits you.

Minimal Fees

Investigate the fees associated with whatever account you're looking into. Look for banks that offer low or no monthly maintenance fees, no minimum balance requirements, and free ATM transactions. Additionally, be wary of overdraft fees, which can be costly. Some banks offer overdraft protection or accounts without overdraft fees.

Digital Features

In today's digital world, having access to online and mobile banking is a must. Check if the bank offers a robust mobile app that allows you to monitor your account, make transfers, deposit checks, and pay bills online. The ease of use of the bank's digital platforms is also very important. A user-friendly interface can make your banking experience much smoother. No one wants to have to deal with a buggy banking app that crashes in the middle of a transaction.

Lifestyle Matches

Consider how a bank's services align with your lifestyle. If you travel frequently, a bank with a national or international presence might be beneficial. If you're into online shopping, look for banks with easy online transaction capabilities.

Credit Unions

Credit unions are nonprofit organizations often providing lower fees and better interest rates. They are member-owned and can offer a more personalized banking experience. Essentially, the way credit unions work is that you become a shareholder once you open an account of your own. This also translates to lower fees and interest rates. Check the eligibility requirements for joining a credit union, as some are based on location, employment, or other affiliations.

Locations and Accessibility

While digital banking is convenient, having access to a local branch can be beneficial. It's easier to get in-person assistance, especially for more complex financial matters. Also, consider the availability and location of ATMs, especially if you prefer using cash. We'll explore the idea of digital versus physical banking in the next section.

Online Banking vs. Branch Banking

Everyone and everything is going digital now! But being a teen, you probably don't need to be told that. You were practically born into a digital world already. In the past, banks existed as physical establishments where people could physically deposit money into designated accounts. Those establishments still exist today, but there's another mode of banking that has emerged in accordance with an increasingly technologically inclined landscape.

Both traditional and online banking have their unique features, advantages, and disadvantages. Understanding these can help you make informed decisions about managing your finances.

Online Banking

Online banking, also known as internet or digital banking, allows you to manage your bank account and perform financial transactions through the bank's website or mobile app. This means you can do most of your banking without ever stepping into a physical bank branch.

Pros:

- **Convenience:** Access your account and conduct transactions anytime, anywhere.
- **Time-Saving:** No need to visit a branch for most banking needs.

- **Easy Monitoring:** Keep a close eye on your account activity, which can help with budgeting and spotting unauthorized transactions quickly.
- **Functionality:** Most online banking platforms offer a range of services, including fund transfers, bill payments, and mobile check deposits.

Cons:

- **Internet Dependency:** Requires a reliable internet connection.
- **Limited Personal Interaction:** This is not ideal if you prefer face-to-face assistance.
- **Security Concerns:** While banks employ robust security measures, online banking can be susceptible to cybersecurity threats like hacking and phishing.

Traditional or Branch Banking

Traditional banking involves visiting a physical bank branch for your financial needs. This is the classic way of banking, where you interact with bank personnel for transactions.

Pros:

- **Personal Service:** Direct interaction with bank staff can be reassuring, especially for complex transactions or issues.
- **Range of Services:** Some services, particularly more complex ones, may only be available or easier to handle in person.
- **Physical Documentation:** Important for those who prefer paper records or are not as tech-savvy.

Cons:

- **Less Convenient:** Requires you to physically visit a branch, often within its operating hours.
- **Time-Consuming:** Potentially longer waiting times and travel involved.
- **Limited Accessibility:** Accessibility can be an issue if you live far from a branch or have mobility challenges.

While both online and branch banking aim to provide financial services, their approaches differ significantly. In terms of accessibility, online banking offers 24/7 access, while branch banking is limited to specific hours. In that sense, online banking has the edge. When it comes to services, it's almost practically a tie. While most common transactions can be done through both, certain specialized services may require a branch visit.

One key advantage of branch banking is personalized service. Branch banking offers more personal interaction, which can be significant for complex financial matters, while online banking offers more autonomy and efficiency. If you're just starting out on your banking journey, having the help of a real service professional can be immensely valuable.

One method isn't necessarily better than the other. Most traditional commercial banks nowadays already offer a digital presence. So, you're getting the best of both worlds with these kinds of banks.

OPENING YOUR FIRST BANK ACCOUNT

Opening your first bank account is not just an exciting milestone but also a significant step into the world of financial independence and responsibility. This moment marks the beginning of your personal finance management, where you start to have control over your own money. However, it's a decision that should be approached with care and consideration.

Choosing the right bank account is more than just picking a place to store your money. It's about finding an account that aligns with your financial needs, goals, and habits. As a teenager, your banking needs might differ from those of adults, and it's important to choose an account that not only meets your current needs but can also grow with you.

What Features to Look for in a Teen Account

As you venture into opening your first bank account, it's essential to understand the different features and aspects that make a bank account suitable for your needs. Here's a breakdown of key features to consider:

Fees

Monthly Maintenance Fees: Some accounts charge a monthly fee just to keep the account open. Look for accounts that don't have this fee or offer easy ways to waive it, like maintaining a minimum balance or having a regular deposit.

ATM Fees: Check if the bank charges fees for using ATMs, especially those outside their network. Some banks offer reimbursement for these fees.

Overdraft Fees: Understand the bank's policy on overdrafts. Some banks offer overdraft protection programs that can prevent hefty fees. *See page 48 for more information on overdrafts*

Security

FDIC Insurance: Ensure that the bank is FDIC insured. This means your deposits are protected up to $250,000, providing security for your money.

Online Security Features: Look for banks that offer robust online security measures like two-factor authentication, fraud monitoring, and secure messaging.

Accessibility

Online and Mobile Banking: Given the importance of digital access, check if the bank offers a comprehensive online banking platform and a mobile app. These tools should allow you to check balances, transfer money, deposit checks, and pay bills.

Branch and ATM Accessibility: Consider how important physical branch access is to you. If you prefer in-person services, look for a bank with branches near your home or school. Also, consider the availability and location of ATMs for easy cash access.

Minimum Balance Requirements

Minimum Opening Deposit: Some banks require a minimum amount to open an account. Look for accounts with low or no minimum opening deposit.

Minimum Balance to Avoid Fees: Be aware of any minimum daily or monthly balance requirements to avoid fees. Aim for accounts with low or no minimum balance requirements to keep things flexible and accessible.

How to Find the Best Bank Account

Okay. You know what features to consider when selecting a bank. Now, it's a matter of figuring out where to look. You might have a few banks with brick-and-mortar branches within your neighborhood that might seem like the obvious choices. But there's more to it than that! Here's how you can approach this process:

Do Your Research on Local Banks

Start Local: Investigate the banks in your area. Local banks might offer advantages such as community involvement, personalized customer service, and easily accessible branches.

Check Offerings: Look at what different local banks offer in terms of teen or student accounts. These accounts are often tailored to younger users and might come with educational resources or special benefits.

Read Reviews and Ratings: Look for customer reviews or ratings online to gauge the reputation and service quality of the local banks.

Compare Bank Accounts

Comparison Chart: Create a chart or list to compare different bank accounts. Include key factors like fees, interest rates, minimum balance requirements, and ATM access.

Special Features: Note any special features or benefits that different banks offer, such as rewards programs, financial education tools, or youth-oriented services.

Terms and Conditions: Pay close attention to the fine print. Understanding terms and conditions can help you avoid unexpected fees or restrictions.

Consider Accessibility

ATM and Branch Network: Consider how important access to physical branches and ATMs is for you. If you travel frequently or prefer cash transactions, a bank with a wide ATM network might be beneficial.

Digital Banking Services: For tech-savvy teens, the quality of digital banking services is crucial. Ensure the bank offers a robust online and mobile banking experience that allows you to manage your finances effectively and securely.

Customer Support: Good customer support is very important, especially for first-time account holders. Check if the bank offers reliable and accessible customer service, including online chat, phone support, and in-branch assistance.

While it may be tempting to walk through the doors of the first bank you see, it's not always going to be the smartest decision. It's important that you don't make any decisions on a whim. You must equip yourself with all the necessary information that will make you feel confident about your banking and financial choices.

What Protections Do Banks Offer to Teens?

When it comes to banking, especially for younger customers, understanding the protections and safeguards that banks offer is something that you can't just overlook. As a teen, it's important to choose a bank that not only meets your financial needs but also provides a secure and supportive banking environment. Consider these details throughout the decision-making process:

- **Financial Education:** Many banks offer financial education resources tailored for teens. These can include online courses, articles, and interactive tools that teach budgeting, saving, investing, and other financial basics. This education is critical in building your financial literacy, helping you make informed decisions and developing healthy money habits.

- **Fraud Protection:** Banks typically provide fraud protection services, which can include monitoring for unusual account activity, fraud alerts, and zero-liability policies for unauthorized transactions. As a teen new to banking, these protections are essential to safeguard your money and personal information from potential fraud or theft.
- **Parental Oversight:** Some teen accounts offer the option for parental oversight. This means a parent or guardian can view account activity, which can reassure you and them. Parental oversight can provide a safety net as you learn to manage your account, ensuring that you have guidance in case of any financial missteps.
- **Parental Control:** Certain teen accounts may come with options for parents to set spending limits or control over certain types of transactions. These controls can help prevent overspending and teach you to manage money within set boundaries, fostering responsible financial behavior.
- **Age-Appropriate Access:** Banks often design their teen accounts to offer age-appropriate access to banking services. This might mean limited access to credit facilities but full access to savings and checking features. Age-appropriate access ensures that you get a banking experience that aligns with your maturity and financial skill level, providing a foundation to build upon as you grow older.

Understanding the Process and Requirements

When you're ready to open your bank account, the last thing that you would want to happen is to be sent home by the bank's relationship managers because you don't have the necessary documents needed to open an account. You must go into this process with a thorough understanding of everything you need to prepare in advance. The best thing to do would be to call these banks in advance or go over their websites for the specific details of their account-opening process. For the most part, these banks all have similar processes. Here's a quick general rundown of what you can expect:

Documents Required for Opening a Bank Account

To open a bank account, you'll typically need to provide several pieces of documentation to verify your identity and residence. Here are the common documents required:

- **Government-Issued Photo ID:** This could be a driver's license, state ID, or passport. It serves as a primary form of identification.
- **Social Security Card or Taxpayer Identification Number (TIN):** You'll need your Social Security Number (SSN) or TIN for tax purposes and identity verification.
- **Passport (if applicable):** For additional or non-U.S. citizen identification, a passport is often accepted.
- **Birth Certificate:** Some banks might require a birth certificate, especially for younger teens who may not have a government-issued photo ID.
- **Proof of Address or Residence:** This could be a school report card, or any official document that shows your name and current address. It's used to verify where you live.

Step-By-Step Process of Opening a Bank Account

1. **Choose the Right Bank and Account Type:** Based on your research and the factors discussed earlier, select a bank and the type of account that best suits your needs.
2. **Gather Your Documents:** Collect all the necessary documents mentioned above. If you're under 18, you might need a parent or guardian to co-open the account.
3. **Visit the Bank or Apply Online:** Depending on the bank, you can either visit a branch in person or apply online. Some banks offer both options.
4. **Fill Out the Application Form:** Complete the application form with your personal and contact information. Be sure to fill it out accurately.
5. **Submit Your Documents:** Provide the necessary documents. If applying online, you may need to upload digital copies.
6. **Read and Understand the Terms and Conditions:** Before finalizing the account, it's important to read and understand

the account's terms and conditions, including fees, interest rates (if any), and account usage guidelines.

7. **Make an Initial Deposit (if required):** Some accounts may require an initial deposit. This can often be done in cash at a branch or via an electronic transfer.

8. **Set Up Online Access:** If available, set up your online banking account. This typically involves creating a username and password and may include setting up security questions.

9. **Finalize Your Account Setup:** Once everything is submitted and approved, your account will be opened. You'll receive your account details and, if applicable, your checkbook and debit card.

10. **Familiarize Yourself with Banking Services:** Take the time to learn about the services and features your new account offers, such as mobile banking, ATM access, and customer support.

CHECKING VS. SAVINGS ACCOUNTS

When you're looking to open your first bank account, two fundamental account types you will come across are checking and savings accounts. Now, which one should you open or look to prioritize? What are the differences, similarities, pros, and cons of each? These are the questions that we'll look to answer in this section.

Checking Accounts

A checking account is like your financial toolkit for everyday transactions. It's designed to handle your day-to-day money activities. These accounts typically come with a debit card, which you can use for purchases and ATM withdrawals. Many also offer check-writing capabilities, which might be useful in certain situations, even in our increasingly digital world. Another key feature is access to online and mobile banking, allowing you to manage your finances on the go.

The primary advantage of a checking account is accessibility. Your money is readily available when you need it, whether for buying a snack or paying for a movie ticket. Checking accounts are designed for frequent use, so they usually don't have restrictions on the number of transactions. Additionally, many checking accounts tailored for teens have low or no minimum balance requirements and may waive monthly fees.

The flip side of a checking account is that it usually doesn't earn much (if any) interest. Your money sits in the account without growing substantially. Also, some accounts might come with monthly maintenance fees or require a minimum balance to avoid these fees.

When choosing a checking account, prioritize one with no monthly fees and no minimum balance requirements. Be aware of the overdraft policies—some accounts offer overdraft protection, which can prevent hefty fees if you accidentally overdraw your account.

Savings Accounts

A savings account, on the other hand, is your financial growth engine, meant for stashing away money and watching it grow over time. These accounts typically offer higher interest rates compared to checking accounts, allowing your savings to accumulate over time. However, they often limit the number of withdrawals or transfers you can make each month, encouraging you to save rather than spend.

The key benefit of a savings account is its ability to earn interest. This means the money you put in grows passively, which can be a great way to build up savings for future expenses like college or a car. It also instills financial discipline, as the limited accessibility discourages impulsive spending.

The limited accessibility can be a drawback if you need to access your money frequently. Also, some savings accounts have minimum balance requirements to maintain the account or earn the maximum interest rate.

The choice between a checking and savings account largely depends on your financial needs and goals. If you need an account for frequent daily transactions, a checking account is suitable. For goals like saving for a large purchase or building an emergency fund, a savings account is more appropriate. Many people benefit from having both by using a checking account for everyday expenses and a savings account for long-term financial goals.

BANKING SERVICES EXPLAINED

Remember that it's not just the type of account that matters; the banking services offered can significantly influence your decision. These services can add convenience, security, and flexibility to your banking experience:

Overdraft Services

An overdraft occurs when you spend more money than you have in your checking account. Overdraft services are designed to cover this shortfall temporarily. Essentially, if you make a transaction that exceeds your account balance, the bank covers the difference. This can prevent a transaction from being declined due to insufficient funds.

The primary advantage is convenience and the assurance that your transactions will go through, even if you momentarily dip below your account balance. This can be particularly helpful in emergencies. However, these services usually come with fees, which can be substantial. Some banks also charge interest on the overdraft amount. It's important to understand the bank's overdraft policies, including any associated fees and repayment terms.

Look for banks that offer overdraft protection with minimal fees. Some banks offer a grace period to repay the overdraft without extra charges, or they might allow linking a savings account to cover overdrafts automatically.

Debit Cards

A debit card is linked directly to your checking account. It allows you to make purchases or withdraw cash up to the amount available in your account. When you make a purchase with a debit card, the amount is deducted directly from your checking account. You can also use it at ATMs for cash withdrawals, deposits, or checking your account balance.

Debit cards offer convenience for making transactions and are widely accepted. They are also a safer alternative to carrying cash. Since the card is linked to your checking account, it's vital to keep track of your balance to avoid overdrafts. Also, unlike credit cards, debit cards generally don't build your credit history.

ATM Services

ATMs (Automated Teller Machines) provide a range of banking services without needing to visit a bank branch. These machines allow you to withdraw cash, deposit checks and cash, transfer money between accounts, and check account balances. They primarily offer convenience, especially for cash withdrawals and simple banking transactions, and are usually available 24/7.

Look for banks with a wide network of ATMs, particularly in locations convenient for you. Some banks reimburse fees incurred at out-of-network ATMs.

USING BANKING APPS

Given that you're a child of the 21st century, mobile apps shouldn't be an alien concept to you. In fact, you probably integrate technology into various aspects of your everyday life almost seamlessly. It should be no different than banking. For this chapter's interactive element, you can go over some of the best banking apps that are designed to help make your financial journey easier, more educational, and even more fun! Check out these banking apps and see which one you like the most:

- **Copper:** Copper is designed specifically for teens and offers an interactive platform to learn about financial management. It includes saving tools and educational content to build financial literacy.
- **Axos Bank First Checking:** This app offers a fee-free checking account designed for teens, providing a debit card and financial tools. It emphasizes security with real-time alerts and parental controls.
- **Chase First Banking:** Developed by Chase, this app is tailored for teens and children with parental involvement. It offers features like setting allowances, spending controls, and savings goals.
- **Greenlight:** Greenlight is more than just a banking app; it's a financial education tool. It allows parents to set controls and

monitor spending while offering teens guidance on money management.

- **FamZoo:** FamZoo specializes in preparing teens for the real world of finance. It includes features for budgeting, saving, and even charitable giving.
- **Capital One MONEY:** This teen-friendly app from Capital One offers fee-free banking, a debit card, and the ability to track spending, set savings goals, and learn about financial management.

In this chapter, you navigated through the essentials of opening bank accounts, understanding different banking services, and even exploring the best banking apps to make your financial journey smooth and efficient. From setting up your accounts to comprehending the ins and outs of financial institutions, you're well on your way to financial mastery.

Now, armed with this newfound knowledge, it's time to dive into another crucial skill in personal finance: budgeting. This next chapter is all about taking control of your finances, ensuring that every dollar you earn, save, or spend is part of a well-thought-out plan.

CHAPTER 5
YOUR BUDGETING BLUEPRINT

Budgeting is not just for people who do not have enough money. It is for everyone who wants to ensure that their money is enough.

ROSETTE MUGIDDE WAMAMBE

BUDGETING IS one of the most important skills you could ever develop, not just in personal finance but in life overall. All in all, budgeting is about understanding how to manage your resources effectively so that you will be able to sustain yourself. In this chapter, we'll cover the fundamental concepts of budgeting, setting the stage for more advanced topics.

Budgeting is more than just a financial task; it's a life skill that empowers you to take control of your money. It's about making conscious choices with your finances and planning for both the expected and unexpected. Whether you're saving for college, managing your earnings from a part-time job, or planning for a big purchase, a well-crafted budget is your roadmap to financial success.

BUDGETING BASICS

A budget is a detailed plan that outlines your expected income and expenses over a certain period, usually a month. Think of it as a financial blueprint; it guides how you allocate your money to various expenses while aiming to save a portion of your income. In simpler terms, it's about planning and tracking where your money comes and goes. Income covers all sources of money you receive, like allowances, job earnings, or any other form of income. Expenses are any costs you incur, including necessities (like food and transportation) and discretionary spending (like entertainment or eating out).

The act of budgeting helps you prioritize your spending. By understanding where your money goes, you can make informed decisions about cutting unnecessary expenses or reallocating funds to more important areas. Additionally, a budget includes a category for savings, encouraging you to set aside a portion of your income regularly. This habit is key for financial security and achieving long-term goals, like a college education or a car purchase.

Without a budget, spending more than you earn is easy, leading to debt. Budgeting helps you live within your means, reducing the likelihood of accumulating debt through overspending. Budgeting is key to reaching financial goals. Whether it's saving for a big trip or investing in your future, a budget helps you allocate resources effectively to realize these ambitions.

YOUR FIRST BUDGET

Essential Components of a Budget

Now, before you can start creating a budget system of your own, it's important that you fully understand the essential components of a proper budget. Your budget should cover all aspects of your financial life. It helps you understand and manage where your money comes from and where it goes. Here are the essential components that should be included in your first budget:

- **Income:** Income is the money you receive regularly. This could be from a part-time job, allowances, gifts, or any other source.
- **Fixed Expenses:** Fixed expenses are recurring costs that generally do not change from month to month. Examples include subscription services, phone bills, or insurance premiums.

- **Debt:** Debt refers to any money you owe, such as loans or credit card balances.
- **Savings:** Savings are the portion of your income you set aside for future use rather than immediately spending.
- **Flexible or Variable Expenses:** Flexible expenses are costs that vary from month to month, such as dining out, entertainment, or shopping.

Steps to Creating Your Budget

As you move forward, you will learn that there are many approaches to creating a budget. Not all budget systems look alike, and that's because people have varying goals and situations. As you try to develop a budget system of your own, you must lock down all the foundational elements. Here are a few steps to help you get started:

Calculate Your Income

The first step in budgeting is to determine your total income. This includes all the money you receive regularly, such as earnings from a part-time job, allowances, gifts, or any other sources. If your income varies each month, calculate an average based on past earnings. Accurately calculating your income clearly shows how much money you have to work with each month. Using your net income (the amount you receive after taxes and other deductions) is important for your budget.

Identify Fixed and Variable Costs

Next, list all your expenses, categorizing them into fixed and variable costs. Fixed costs are those that remain constant each month, like rent, subscriptions, or car insurance. Variable costs, on the other hand, fluctuate and include things like dining out, entertainment, and shopping. Identifying these costs helps you understand where your money is going and which areas offer flexibility for adjustments.

Set Up Savings Goals

Setting savings goals is a critical part of budgeting. Determine what you are saving for, whether it's a long-term goal like college, a short-term goal like buying a new gadget, or an emergency fund for unforeseen expenses. Decide how much you want to save each month towards these goals. Treating your savings like a fixed expense ensures that you consistently set money aside.

Allocate Income to Needs, Wants, and Savings

Divide your income into three main categories: needs, wants, and savings. Needs include essential expenses like food and housing; wants are non-essential expenses like entertainment; savings are funds you set aside for future use. This step is about balancing these aspects while ensuring that your needs are covered, setting aside money for savings, and using the remainder for wants.

Decide on Budgeting Categories

Finally, break down your expenses into specific budgeting categories. These can include clothing, personal care, car insurance, cellphone coverage, gas money, entertainment, dining out, etc. Allocating specific amounts to each category helps you manage your spending more effectively. Be realistic in your allocations, and remember to review and adjust these categories as needed based on your actual spending and changing needs.

Tips to Stick to a Budget

Sticking to a budget is a critical skill in managing your finances effectively. It's true that maintaining discipline in budgeting isn't always easy, especially when unexpected expenses arise or when temptations to overspend come your way. However, with the right strategies and mindset, it becomes more manageable. Here are some tips to help you stay on track with your budget:

- **Make Budget Goals Realistic:** Set achievable goals that align with your income and lifestyle. Unrealistic goals can lead to frustration and may cause you to abandon your budget altogether.
- **Try a New Budget Challenge:** Introduce fun challenges to your budgeting routine. For example, try a no-spend week, where you only spend money on essentials, or a progressive saving challenge, where you save a little more each week or month.

- **Know What You're Saving For:** Having a clear purpose for your savings can be a powerful motivator. Knowing what you're working towards makes it easier to stick to your budget.
- **Make a Weekly or Monthly Food Budget:** Food can be a significant expense. Planning your meals and setting a specific budget for groceries can help you avoid overspending.
- **Give Yourself an Allowance for Splurging:** It's important to allow yourself some room in your budget for enjoyment. Set aside a small portion of your budget for splurges. This way, you can indulge occasionally without feeling guilty or derailing your financial plan.

NEEDS VS. WANTS

Do you really need those new pair of Air Jordans? Do you really need that trendy handbag that everyone seems to be carrying around these days? Do you need to splurge on the latest video games? Or do you just *want* these things?

Understanding the difference between needs and wants is a pivotal aspect of budgeting, especially for teens just starting to manage their finances. This distinction helps in making informed decisions about spending and saving, ensuring that essential expenses are prioritized while still allowing room for personal enjoyment.

Needs are essentially... well, the essentials. They are the things you must have to live and function. They typically include food, shelter, basic clothing, healthcare, and education. For a teen, this might translate to school supplies, a bus pass for transportation, or essential clothing. On the other hand, wants are things that enhance your life but are not essential for survival or basic functioning. They can include the latest gadgets, designer clothes, eating out at fancy restaurants, or subscriptions to entertainment services.

The challenge lies in the fact that what may be a need for one person could be a want for another, depending on their circumstances and lifestyle. For instance, a phone might be a need for a teen who uses it for educational purposes but a want for someone who desires the latest model for entertainment.

Budgeting for Needs and Wants

When creating your budget, ensure that your needs are covered first. This ensures that your essential expenses are taken care of before anything else. After setting aside money for needs and savings, you can allocate a portion of your budget for wants. This is where you can express your personal preferences and enjoy the fruits of your financial discipline. The key is finding a balance. Overspending on wants can jeopardize your ability to cover needs or save for future goals. Conversely, spending only on needs might be unrealistic and unsustainable, leading to budget burnout.

BUDGETING STRATEGIES: CHOOSING THE RIGHT ONE FOR YOU

Adopting the right budgeting strategy is key to managing your finances effectively. Again, not everyone will handle their money in the same way, and that's fine. It's about finding the best method for your personality and goals. Each method has a unique approach and can suit different financial habits and goals. Let's explore some popular budgeting strategies to help you determine which one might be the best fit for you:

50/30/20 Budgeting

This simple and intuitive method involves dividing your after-tax income into three categories: 50% for needs, 30% for wants, and 20% for savings or debt repayment.

Allocate 50% of your income to essential expenses like housing, groceries, and transportation. Then, 30% can be used for discretionary spending such as dining out, hobbies, or entertainment. Finally, dedicate 20% to savings or paying off debts (if you have any).

This method is great for beginners or those who want a straightforward and balanced approach to budgeting. It's particularly useful if you're new to managing money and need clear guidelines on how to distribute your income.

Pay Yourself First

'Pay Yourself First' means prioritizing savings by setting aside a portion of your income for savings goals as soon as you receive it before covering other expenses. The way it works is that you have to decide on a percentage of your income to save each month. As soon as you receive your income, immediately transfer this amount to a savings account. Then, use the remaining money to cover your expenses.

This strategy is ideal if you're focused on building your savings, whether for an emergency fund, a specific purchase, or long-term financial goals. It ensures that saving is a priority, not an afterthought.

Zero-Based Budget

In a zero-based budget, you allocate every dollar of your income to specific expenses, savings, and debt payments, so your income minus your expenditures equals zero. You have to list all sources of income and all expenses, including savings and debt repayments. Then, allocate funds from your income to each expense category until there is no unallocated income left.

This method suits those who want a detailed and hands-on approach to budgeting. It's effective for close monitoring where every dollar goes and can be particularly useful if you're working with a tight budget.

Envelope Budgeting

Lastly, there's envelope budgeting. This is a tangible, hands-on method where you use physical envelopes to manage your spending in different categories. Label envelopes with different spending categories (like groceries, entertainment, etc.). After that, allocate cash in each envelope as per your budget. Once the cash in an envelope is gone, you stop spending in that category until the next budget period.

This strategy is excellent for those who prefer dealing with cash and need a very disciplined approach to limit spending. It's especially effective for managing variable expenses and avoiding overspending.

BUDGET TEMPLATES FOR GOOGLE SHEETS

One of the most efficient ways to manage your budget is by using tools like Google Sheets or Excel. These platforms offer flexibility, automation, and easy tracking of your finances. For teens embarking on their budgeting journey, these tools can simplify the process and make it more interactive. Here's a simple and fool-proof way to develop your own budgeting sheet:

1. **Open a New Spreadsheet:** Start by opening Google Sheets or Excel and create a new spreadsheet.
2. **Create Income and Expense Categories:** At the top of the spreadsheet, list your income sources. Below that, create categories for your expenses, such as 'Food,' 'Transportation,' 'Entertainment,' etc.
3. **Input Monthly Figures:** Enter the amount you expect to receive or spend each month in the respective categories. For variable expenses, you can use an average based on past spending.
4. **Add Formulas for Totaling:** Use formulas to automatically calculate your total income, total expenses, and the difference between the two. This helps you see at a glance whether you are living within your means.
5. **Track Actual Spending:** As the month progresses, input your actual spending next to your estimated figures. This will help you identify areas where you're overspending or underspending.
6. **Adjust as Needed:** At the end of each month, review your budget and make adjustments for the next month based on your actual spending habits and changing needs.

If you're not so keen on developing a template from scratch, that's fine. There are a bunch of templates that you can use online that you can customize according to your needs. Google offers a variety of budget templates that you can find in the template gallery of Google Sheets. Look for templates labeled as 'Personal budget,' 'Monthly budget,' or something similar. You can do the same for Microsoft Excel as well!

And that does it for our chapter on budgeting. Now, you should have a better sense of control over your finances. In the next chapter, we'll expand on that sense of control even further by delving deeper into the world of savings.

MAKE A DIFFERENCE WITH YOUR REVIEW

Unlock the Power of Generosity

Hey there, awesome reader! Did you know that people who give without expecting anything in return often lead longer, happier lives? That sounds pretty cool, right? Well, I've got an exciting challenge for you.

Here's the deal: Most people decide which book to read based on its cover and what others say about it. So, I have a small favor to ask for a teen you haven't met yet:

Could you please leave a review for this book?

It won't cost you a dime and will take less than a minute, but your words could change another teen's life forever. Your review could be the reason why...

- Another young person starts saving for their future.
- A future entrepreneur gets inspired to start a business.
- Someone learns to budget and spend wisely.
- A dream of financial independence becomes a reality.

Ready to feel awesome and help out? Here's what you need to do (it's super quick!):

Just leave a review.

Point your phone's camera at this QR code to share your thoughts:

A big thank you from the heart. Now, let's jump back into our fun financial journey.

Your friend, Freddie Grant

P.S. - Cool fact: When you help someone, you become more valuable to them. Think this book could help another teen? Share it with them, and spread the goodness!

CHAPTER 6
THE SAVINGS CODE

Do not save what is left after spending, but spend what is left after saving.

WARREN BUFFETT

AS A TEEN, learning to save effectively is more than just setting money aside; it's about laying the groundwork for your financial future. In this chapter, we delve into the essential skills and strategies for cultivating a robust savings habit. You can expect to understand the basic principles of saving and why it's a critical component of financial health. Together, we can uncover practical strategies to develop and maintain a habit of regular saving, regardless of your income level. This chapter will help you explore various savings options available to you, including traditional savings accounts, certificates of deposit, and more, to find what best suits your needs.

WHY START SAVING NOW?

One of the first lessons in saving is learning the value of every dollar. For teens, this is an important concept. When you start saving, you begin to understand how much effort it takes to earn each dollar and the importance of using it wisely. This understanding fosters a sense of financial responsibility and mindfulness about spending. It helps you discern between impulsive purchases and thoughtful expenditures, making every dollar count towards something meaningful or necessary.

Developing a savings habit early on is also a fundamental step in learning how to stay out of debt. If you set aside a portion of any money you receive, you create a financial buffer. This buffer can be essential for unexpected expenses, reducing the need to borrow money or use credit, which can lead to debt. Understanding and practicing this can help you avoid the pitfalls of overspending and accruing unnecessary debts, which is especially important as you transition into adulthood.

Ultimately, the earlier you start saving, the quicker it becomes a habit. Starting young gives you a considerable advantage; it allows you to integrate saving into your daily life as a regular practice. Like any habit, the more you do it, the more ingrained it becomes. This habitual saving sets a strong foundation for financial discipline, benefiting you throughout your life.

Another significant advantage of starting to save early is the journey towards self-reliance. This kind of independence is empowering as it brings confidence in your ability to handle money and make decisions that positively impact your financial future. It also prepares you for greater financial responsibilities that come with adulthood.

Finally, an important aspect of saving early is the benefit of compound interest. Compound interest is essentially "interest on interest." It occurs when the interest earned on your savings is reinvested, and you earn additional interest on the new total. Over time, this compounding effect can significantly increase your savings. The earlier you start saving, the more time your money has to grow through compound interest, magnifying the rewards of your early financial discipline. We'll talk more about the magic of compound interest in our chapter on investing.

SETTING SAVINGS GOALS

Savings goals are specific financial objectives you aim to achieve by saving money. These goals give purpose and direction to your savings efforts, transforming the act of setting money aside into a strategic and meaningful endeavor. Essentially, savings goals are the 'why' behind your savings. They're what motivate you to save a portion of your income consistently.

Teens might have a variety of savings goals, depending on their interests, needs, and aspirations. Here are some common examples:

- **Educational Expenses:** Many teens save for future educational costs, like college tuition, textbooks, or other school-related expenses. This goal is particularly important for those looking to lessen the financial burden of higher education.
- **Technology Upgrades:** In an era where technology is integral to both education and social life, saving up for the latest phone, laptop, or other gadgets is a common goal among teens.
- **Transportation:** This could include saving for a car, including the purchase price, insurance, and maintenance costs, or even saving for a bike or public transportation passes.
- **Entertainment and Recreation:** Teens also save for leisure activities, such as attending concerts, going on a trip with friends, or buying gaming consoles.
- **Personal Projects:** Some teens might save for personal projects or hobbies, such as starting a small business, funding an art project, or buying sports equipment.

Setting savings goals is crucial because it gives your financial efforts a clear direction and purpose. When you save without a specific goal, it can be challenging to stay motivated and disciplined. However, with a defined objective, you're more likely to be committed and make thoughtful decisions about your spending and saving habits. Goals turn the abstract concept of saving into tangible targets, making it easier to visualize progress and success.

Here are a few tips on how you can stay on top of your savings goals:

- **Set a Savings Deadline:** Establishing a timeframe for your goal creates a sense of urgency and helps maintain focus. Whether it's saving for a concert ticket in three months or a car in a few years, deadlines help you structure your saving plan and keep you on track.

- **Choose a Specific Savings Goal:** Be as specific as possible with your goals. Instead of a vague aim like "save more money," opt for a clear target like "save $500 for a new laptop." Specific goals are easier to manage and measure.
- **Create a Different Account for Each Goal:** Consider opening separate savings accounts for different goals. This separation makes tracking your progress for each objective easier and prevents you from accidentally using funds allocated for one goal on another.
- **Track Your Goals:** Regularly monitor your progress. This could be as simple as checking your savings balance or using a budgeting app to track how close you are to achieving your goal. Seeing your progress can be a great motivator.
- **Break Goals Down into Smaller Milestones:** Large goals can seem daunting. Break them down into smaller, more manageable milestones. For example, if you're saving $1,200 for a trip, aim to save $100 each month over the course of a year. These smaller steps make the goal feel more achievable and keep you motivated.

Again, having clear savings goals helps you stay focused and disciplined with your finances. It's about envisioning a future need or desire and planning your savings accordingly. This forward-thinking approach ensures that you're not just saving for the sake of saving but rather with a specific outcome in mind.

BUILDING AN EMERGENCY FUND

An emergency fund is often considered one of the most critical savings goals for anyone, regardless of age or financial status. It acts as a financial safety net that can help you navigate unexpected situations without derailing your budget or plunging you into debt. Life is full of surprises, and having an emergency fund ensures that you are better prepared to handle them financially.

An emergency fund is money you set aside for unplanned expenses or financial emergencies. These can include sudden medical bills, unexpected car repairs, or unforeseen educational expenses. The primary importance of an emergency fund is its role in providing financial security. In the event of an unexpected expense, you can rely on this fund instead of using credit cards or loans, which can lead to high-interest debt. It also offers peace of mind, knowing you have a cushion to fall back on in tough times.

How Much Should Be Saved for an Emergency Fund?

A common recommendation is to save enough to cover three to six months' worth of living expenses. This amount gives you a substantial buffer to handle most emergencies. The ideal size of your emergency fund can vary based on your personal circumstances, such as your job stability, monthly expenses, and whether you have dependents. Start by aiming for a smaller, more achievable goal, like saving $500 or $1,000, and then gradually increase it over time.

Where Do You Store Your Emergency Fund?

Your emergency fund should be easily accessible and stored in a safe place. This usually means keeping it in a savings account, where it's not subject to market risks and can be withdrawn quickly when needed. Additionally, it's wise to keep your emergency fund separate from your regular checking or savings accounts. This separation helps to avoid the temptation of dipping into these funds for non-emergency expenses.

What Counts as an Emergency?

The key rule for an emergency fund is to use it only in actual emergencies. These are situations that are urgent, necessary, and unexpected. It's not for planned expenses or discretionary spending. This could cover anything from unexpected hospital admissions and medical emergencies to car troubles or home repairs, or even losing your job. After using funds from your emergency account, make it a priority to replenish it. This ensures that you're prepared for any future emergencies.

SAVING FOR MULTIPLE GOALS

When it comes to saving, one size doesn't fit all, especially when you have multiple goals with varying timelines. Whether it's a short-term goal like buying a new phone, a medium-range goal like saving for a car, or a long-term goal like college tuition, each requires a different approach. Here's how you can strategically save for multiple goals simultaneously:

Befriend Automation!

Automating your savings is a powerful strategy. You can set up automatic transfers from your checking account to your savings account(s). This ensures that you consistently save a portion of your income without having to think about it every time. Most banks offer the option to set up automatic transfers on a schedule that works for you – it could be weekly, bi-weekly, or monthly. Align these transfers with your payday to make the process seamless.

Categorize Your Goals

Each type of goal requires a different saving strategy. Short-term goals might require more aggressive saving over a shorter period, while long-term goals can be approached with a slower, steady saving plan. Also, determine which goals are most urgent or important to you and allocate your savings accordingly. For example, if you're aiming to buy a new laptop for school (short-term), start saving for a car (medium-range), and put money away for college (long-term), decide how much of your savings to allocate to each goal based on their priority and timeline.

Make Use of Multiple Savings Accounts

Having separate savings accounts for each goal can help you stay organized and track your progress more efficiently. This separation ensures that you don't accidentally use funds meant for one goal for another. Many banks allow you to label or nickname your accounts. This can be a helpful way to remind yourself what each account is for, like "Car Fund" or "College Savings."

Stay Organized

Regularly check the balances of your savings accounts to see how you're progressing toward each goal. This can also help you adjust your saving amounts if you're falling short or if you're able to save more. Don't be afraid to make adjustments along the way, either. Life changes, and so may your goals and financial situation. Periodically review your goals and the amount you're saving towards each to ensure they still align with your current needs and priorities.

HOW TO SAVE FOR SOMETHING YOU REALLY WANT

Of course, you're entitled to want to spend on things that others might deem impractical. That's okay. You should be able to do whatever you want with your money as long as you don't hurt others, right? Part of being financially responsible is learning how to save up for things that you actually want, be it a new gaming console, a bike, concert tickets, or even a trip with friends. Here's how you can go about doing so:

- **Know How Much You Need to Save:** The first step is determining how much the item or experience you want costs. This includes the base price and any additional expenses like taxes, shipping, or accessories. Knowing the exact amount you need makes your saving goal tangible and measurable. It gives you a clear target to work towards, which can be incredibly motivating.
- **Know What to Set Aside:** Once you have your target number, break it down into smaller, manageable saving increments. For example, if you need $300 for a new phone and have six months to save, you'll need to set aside $50 each month. Incorporate this saving amount into your monthly budget. Treat it like a fixed expense, similar to how you would handle a bill or a subscription.
- **Save Without Thinking About It:** Set up an automatic transfer from your checking account to your savings account for the amount you need to save each month. Automating the process ensures that you consistently save without having to remember to transfer the money manually.

- **Make the Necessary Sacrifices:** Look for non-essential expenses you can cut back on, like eating out, subscription services you don't use often, or impulse buys. It's always important to make conscious decisions about your spending. For instance, if you usually buy lunch at school, consider packing a lunch from home and saving the difference.
- **Increase Your Income Sources:** If saving from your current income isn't enough, look for ways to make extra money. This could be through a part-time job, freelancing, doing odd jobs, or selling items you no longer need. Any extra money you make, whether it's from birthday money, a bonus from a part-time job, or money from selling old video games, can go straight into your savings for this particular goal.

SAVING OPTIONS

You now have a good idea of how to build a proper savings habit. In this section, we'll discuss the different options that are available to you when it comes to depositing your savings. Each option has its own fair share of features and benefits, so don't be afraid to explore and experiment. Remember that it's a good idea to mix different saving platforms for different saving goals.

Online Savings Account

Online savings accounts are a modern twist on traditional savings methods. Operated entirely through digital platforms without physical branch networks, they typically offer higher interest rates due to lower overhead costs. These accounts are ideal for tech-savvy savers comfortable with managing their finances online. The benefits include higher returns on your savings, often lower fees, and the convenience of handling your finances from anywhere. These accounts are best suited for those who prioritize high-interest rates and do not require in-person banking services.

Regular Savings Account

Regular savings accounts are the most common type provided by traditional banks. These accounts are straightforward, allowing you to deposit and withdraw money relatively easily. They are characterized by their accessibility and low entry barriers, often having low or no minimum balance requirements. While their interest rates might be lower than other savings options, they offer simplicity and ease of access to funds, making them a suitable choice for individuals looking for a no-frills place to keep their savings.

High-Yield Savings Account

High-yield savings accounts are similar to regular savings accounts but stand out due to their significantly higher interest rates. They are an excellent option for long-term savings goals, as the higher interest rates allow your money to grow more rapidly over time. These accounts are particularly beneficial for savers who have a stable financial situation and can afford to leave their money untouched to accrue interest over longer periods.

Certificates of Deposit (CDs)

Certificates of Deposit (CDs) are time-bound savings products with a fixed interest rate and a fixed term of maturity. The duration can range from a few months to several years. The main advantage of CDs is that they usually offer higher interest rates compared to traditional savings accounts. However, they require you to lock in your money for a set period, making them less flexible in terms of access to funds. CDs are ideal for savers with long-term goals who do not need immediate access to their money.

Money Market Account

Money market accounts blend the features of savings and checking accounts. They offer higher interest rates like savings accounts but also provide some checking account features like check-writing and debit card access. These accounts are suitable for individuals who seek a higher return on their savings but also want more accessibility to their funds than what CDs offer.

Student Savings Account

Student savings accounts are tailored specifically for the needs of student savers. These accounts often come with benefits like no or low minimum balance requirements, no monthly fees, and sometimes, educational resources about managing personal finances. They are designed to be student-friendly, making them a great starting point for young individuals beginning their financial journey.

Savings Account with Auto-Saving Features

Some savings accounts come equipped with an auto-savings feature. This allows you to set up automatic, recurring transfers from your checking account to your savings account. It automates the process of saving, ensuring regular contributions to your savings without the need for manual transfers each time. These accounts are perfect for those who want to build a savings habit effortlessly.

30-DAY SAVINGS CHALLENGE

Why don't we get started on your savings habit as early as now? After all, people always say that the best time to start saving is yesterday! For an easy way of kickstarting your savings habit, follow these steps:

1. **Set a Goal:** Start by setting a clear and specific savings goal for the month. It could be anything from saving for a new pair of sneakers to starting your emergency fund.
2. **Establish a Starting Point:** Assess your financial situation and determine how much you can realistically set aside each day. Remember, the key is consistency, not the amount.
3. **Create a Daily Savings Plan:** Divide your total monthly savings goal by 30 to find out how much you need to save each day. Make sure this daily amount is challenging yet achievable.
4. **Find a Savings Container:** Decide where you'll keep your saved money. It could be a traditional piggy bank, a savings jar, or a dedicated digital savings account. Choose what excites you and aligns with your saving style.
5. **Commit to Being Consistent:** The success of this challenge hinges on your commitment to save the determined amount every single day. Consistency is more important than the amount saved.
6. **Track Your Progress:** Keep a daily record of your savings. You can use a notebook, a spreadsheet, or a budgeting app to track how much you're setting aside each day.

7. **Celebrate Milestones:** Celebrate when you reach significant points in your challenge, like the first week, the halfway point, or when you've saved a certain amount. These celebrations serve as motivation to continue.
8. **Reflect on the Journey:** At the end of the 30 days, reflect on what you've learned and achieved. Consider how this challenge has impacted your view of saving and spending.

An important reminder: This 30-day savings challenge is not just about the amount you save; it's about building the discipline and habit of saving. It's a practical exercise that can have a lasting impact on your financial behavior.

As we wrap up with this challenge and your exciting journey into the world of savings, let's pivot to our next chapter: Savvy Spending. It's not just about the money that you manage to earn and keep. It's also about learning how to spend *wisely*. Life without expenses is unrealistic. However, learning how to spend intelligently is the key to financial freedom.

CHAPTER 7
SAVVY SPENDING

He who buys what he does not need steals from himself.

SWEDISH PROVERB

AS YOUNG INDIVIDUALS stepping into the world of financial independence, understanding how to make smart spending decisions is as important as learning to save. Savvy spending isn't just about cutting costs or limiting yourself; it's about making each expenditure count and aligning your spending habits with your financial goals and values. This chapter will equip you with the skills and knowledge to navigate the myriad of spending decisions you face daily, from choosing where to shop to deciding if an item is worth its price.

MASTERING THE ART OF SMART SHOPPING

Shopping is an inevitable part of our lives and is not inherently detrimental to our finances. In fact, when done smartly, it can be a rewarding experience that aligns perfectly with savvy spending habits. This section is dedicated to helping you navigate the world of shopping in a financially responsible way and aligned with your goals. These habits will help you enjoy the process of buying what you need or want without derailing your financial plans.

Create a Dedicated Shopping Account

Consider setting up a separate checking account specifically for shopping. This can help you manage your spending by allocating a fixed budget for shopping, preventing overspending. Aside from making it easier to track your shopping expenses, a dedicated shopping account keeps your primary account reserved for essential expenditures.

Leave Credit Cards at Home

When you shop with a credit card, spending more than you intended is easy. By leaving your credit cards at home and using cash or a debit card, you limit yourself to spending only what you have. This practice encourages you to think more critically about each purchase, as you're directly dealing with the money you have available.

Research Reviews

Before making a purchase, especially for more expensive items, read reviews from other consumers. This can give you a better idea of the product's quality and value for money. Reviews can help you avoid buying products that don't meet your expectations or needs, saving you from wasted expenditures.

Stack Coupons When Available

Look for and utilize coupons to get discounts on items you need. Stacking coupons or using more than one coupon for a single item can lead to significant savings. Keep an eye on coupon websites, store flyers, and emails for potential deals. Additionally, you can use the browser extension, Rakuten, which pays you cashback for purchases on many websites.

Get Stores' Apps

Many stores have mobile apps that offer exclusive deals, digital coupons, and personalized discounts. These apps can also make the shopping process more efficient and tailored to your preferences.

Sign Up for Rewards Programs

Rewards and loyalty programs can offer cashback, points, or discounts on future purchases. If you frequently shop at certain stores, these programs can be a great way to get more value out of your spending.

Compare Prices

Before making a purchase, compare prices online, in different stores, and with competitors. Sometimes, significant price differences can be found for the same item. Or use a browser extension like Camelcamelcamel, that compares prices on a specific item on Amazon over time, so you know when you're buying it at it's cheapest.

Find Discount Codes

Look for discount codes on websites, newsletters, or browser extensions (like Honey). These codes can offer substantial discounts, especially for online purchases.

Limit Online Shopping

Online shopping can be incredibly convenient but also makes impulsive buying easier. Set limits on your online shopping habits to avoid overspending.

DEALING WITH IMPULSE PURCHASES

Have you ever tried casually strolling through the mall, and one item in the store window catches your eye? You walk in, check the price tag, and are told it's on sale. Naturally, you tell yourself that you're saving money by buying it now because of the discounted price. You walk right up to the cashier and ask them to check your item out. You walk out of the store believing that you got a good deal, and you're feeling pretty pleased with yourself. That right there is a perfect example of impulse buying.

Impulse purchases are unplanned buying decisions made on the spur of the moment without prior intention or consideration. These are often characterized by a sudden, strong urge to buy something immediately, typically driven by emotions rather than need or careful thought. For you, in the early stages of learning financial responsibility, understanding and managing impulse purchases is super beneficial.

Why Do People Impulse Buy?

- **Peer Pressure:** For teens, peer influence can strongly drive impulse buying. Seeing friends with the latest fashion items, gadgets, or other trendy purchases can create a sense of urgency to keep up.

- **Past Experiences:** Sometimes, past shopping experiences can trigger impulse buying. If buying something previously led to positive feelings, one might be inclined to replicate that experience without thorough consideration.
- **Discounts/Marketing:** Marketing strategies and discounts can create a sense of scarcity or a 'deal too good to miss.' Retailers often use sales tactics that can lead to impulsive buying decisions, like limited-time offers or buy-one-get-one-free deals.
- **Shopping Addiction:** In some cases, impulse buying can be part of a larger pattern of shopping addiction, where the act of buying provides a temporary emotional high or escape.
- **Instant Gratification:** The desire for instant gratification—wanting to experience pleasure or fulfillment without delay—is a common reason behind impulse purchases. The immediate satisfaction of acquiring something new can be a powerful motivator to buy impulsively.

Tips to Quit Impulse Buying

Impulse buying can be a hard habit to break, especially when buying something you want feels gratifying. However, with the right strategies, gaining control over these spontaneous purchases is possible. Here are some effective tips to help curb impulse buying:

- **Stick to a Budget:** A well-defined budget is one of the most effective ways to prevent impulse buying. When you allocate your money to specific categories, it's easier to resist spending on items that aren't part of your plan.
- **Pause Before Purchasing:** When you feel the urge to make an unplanned purchase, apply the 24-hour rule. Wait for 24 hours before buying the item. Often, this time allows the initial impulse to fade, and you can assess whether you really need or want the item.
- **Extend the Waiting Period:** For more expensive items, extend the waiting period beyond 24 hours. Give yourself a week or even a month to think it over. This waiting period can help

you differentiate between a genuine need and a fleeting want.

- **Find Alternatives to Splurging:** Identify ways to reward or treat yourself that don't involve spending money. This could be spending time on a hobby, enjoying nature, or engaging in a favorite activity.
- **Join an Accountability Group:** Consider joining or forming a group with friends or family who are also trying to save or spend wisely. Sharing your goals and progress can provide mutual support and accountability.
- **Be Aware of Emotional Spending:** Recognize if emotions like stress, boredom, or sadness often trigger your spending. Awareness of these triggers can help you develop healthier responses to these emotions.

Again, impulse buying might feel gratifying, but it's also incredibly dangerous when you're trying to get your finances on track. It's always best to act intentionally and methodically when it comes to your spending. Don't just act on a whim. After all, you work hard and wait patiently for your money. You don't want to go just spending it recklessly in a matter of seconds!

MASTER ONLINE SHOPPING

The world has gone digital, and online shopping has become a staple of our daily lives, offering unparalleled convenience and a vast array of choices at our fingertips. However, this ease of access can also lead to overspending, as the barriers that might exist in physical shopping are virtually non-existent online. Mastering online shopping is about being strategic and mindful to make the most of its conveniences without falling into the trap of impulsive buying. Take note of these tips to ensure that you stay a savvy shopper:

- **Avoid Shopping at Night:** Nighttime can often be when our defenses are down, perhaps due to tiredness or the relaxation of evening hours. It's easy to make impulsive purchases during this time. Try to shop online during the day when you're more alert and less prone to making impulsive decisions.

- **Manage Your Payment Methods Intelligently:** Instead of saving your payment information on shopping sites, manually enter your details each time you make a purchase. This extra step gives you more time to consider each purchase. Also, use debit cards or prepaid cards for online shopping. These payment methods can help you spend only the money you have, unlike credit cards, which can lead to overspending.
- **Use Comparison Tools:** Utilize online comparison tools and apps to compare prices across different websites. This ensures you get the best deal and can save you money. Comparison tools can also provide product reviews and ratings, helping you make more informed choices about the quality and value of what you're buying.

Ultimately, being an intelligent shopper is about exercising control and being deliberate in purchasing decisions. When you are more mindful and intentional with your purchases, staying disciplined and aligned with your goals becomes a lot easier.

TRACKING WEEKLY EXPENSES

One of the most effective ways to enhance your savvy spending skills is by actively identifying and cutting back on unnecessary expenses. Let's turn this into an immersive week-long challenge. This exercise not only helps you save money but also brings greater awareness to your spending patterns.

1. **Identify Unnecessary Expenses:** Track every penny you spend for the first couple of days. Look for expenses that are not essential – like daily coffee runs, online purchases of items you don't really need, or subscriptions you rarely use.
2. **Set a Goal:** Decide which non-essential expenses you will cut for the rest of the week. It could be anything from dining out to entertainment costs.
3. **Track Your Progress:** Throughout the week, keep a record of your spending, focusing on the expenses you've decided to cut. Notice how refraining from these expenses impacts your overall financial picture.

4. **Reflect at the End of the Week:** After the week is over, reflect on the experience. How much did you save? Did you find certain cuts more challenging than others? What did you learn about your spending habits?

Best Expense Trackers

Consider using one of the following expense-tracking apps to aid in this challenge. These apps can simplify the process of monitoring your spending and provide insights into where your money goes:

- **YNAB (You Need A Budget):** This app is great for those who want a hands-on approach to budgeting. It encourages users to give every dollar a job, making it ideal for tracking and cutting expenses.
- **PocketGuard:** With a user-friendly interface, PocketGuard helps you keep track of your spending and offers insights on where you might be able to cut back.
- **Goodbudget:** Based on the envelope budgeting method, this app helps allocate your spending into different categories, making it easier to identify and control unnecessary expenses.

Note: Budgeting apps change frequently, so be sure to research the best ones by reading reviews.

Again, don't be afraid of integrating technology into your financial habits! These apps are incredibly effective at helping you achieve your goals without straying away from the path that you're supposed to be on with your finances. In the next chapter, we're now going to segue into a different kind of expense: a good one. We'll learn all about the world of investing and how to make your money work for you.

CHAPTER 8
BUILD YOUR FUTURE FORTUNE THROUGH INVESTING

Investing puts money to work. The only reason to save money is to invest it.

GRANT CARDONE

TO MANY, investing is perceived as a complex activity reserved for adults or those already established in their careers. However, this chapter is here to demystify that notion and introduce you, as a teen, to the empowering world of investing.

Investing is not just about having large sums of money or extensive financial knowledge; it's about understanding how to make your money work for you over the long term. Even with a small amount, wise investments can grow significantly over time, thanks to the power of compound interest and market growth. Now, you might not understand any of these concepts yet, and that's precisely what this chapter is for. Here, we will seek to understand the fundamental concepts of investing, including different types of investments like stocks, bonds, and mutual funds. Ultimately, this chapter is about equipping you with the knowledge and confidence to start making informed investment decisions, setting the foundation for a financially secure future.

INVESTING EXPLAINED

A 15-year-old girl named Vanessa once set up a lemonade stand in her neighborhood. With $10 from her savings, she bought lemons, sugar, and paper cups. Vanessa worked hard, squeezing lemons and mixing her special recipe. By the end of the day, she had earned $30!

Excited, Vanessa faced a choice: she could spend her earnings on a new video game or reinvest in her lemonade business. After some thought, Vanessa decided to reinvest. She bought more supplies and even a second-hand table to attract more customers. The next weekend, Vanessa earned $60.

Seeing the potential, Vanessa continued to reinvest her earnings. She added cookies to her menu, set up a canopy for shade, and even hired her friend, Sam, to help. Her stand became more and more popular, and her earnings grew each week.

Months later, Vanessa had a bustling little business. She saved a significant amount of money, much more than she initially invested. She realized that by reinvesting her earnings, she had made her initial $10 grow exponentially. Vanessa learned a valuable lesson about investing: putting money into a venture can generate more money in the future.

This simple story of Vanessa and her lemonade stand illustrates how investing works. When you invest money, you're allowing it to grow by being part of a business or venture. Essentially, investing is the act of taking money and putting it into a specific vehicle that's designed for growth. This can typically be done by investing in business ventures like Vanessa did. But it can also be done by investing in other vehicles like stocks, bonds, and mutual funds.

BENEFITS OF EARLY INVESTMENT

As a teenager, investing might be the farthest thing from your mind. After all, it's not *normal* for people your age to talk about stocks, bonds, and mutual funds, right? Your peers might be more interested in talking about celebrity gossip, sports news, or developments in fashion trends. You aren't poring over stock indexes right away when you log onto your computer, and that's fine! Be a kid. But you should know that learning to invest early has its fair share of upsides. So, even though it might not be *cool* yet, you might want to learn more about the benefits of early investment:

Compound Interest Benefits

The concept of compound interest is often referred to as the eighth wonder of the world and for a good reason. It's the process where the interest you earn on your investments is reinvested, thereby earning more interest. This cycle continues, leading to exponential growth over time. For teens, the true advantage lies in the time you have on your side. Starting to invest early means that even small amounts of money can grow significantly over the years. This compounding effect becomes more powerful with each passing year, transforming modest savings into substantial sums.

For example, suppose you had $1,000 and put that in a savings account where it wasn't gaining any interest. You then continued to save an additional $100 every month in that account. At the end of 10 years, you'd have $13,000 in the account. Not bad!

But, if instead, you invest that $1,000 in stocks at an average annual rate of 8% (which is a reasonable average return) and contribute an additional $100 every month by the end of 10 years, you'd have a total of $20,514. That's a big difference. And thanks to compound interest, the longer you keep the money invested at that rate, it will continue to grow exponentially! At the end of 20 years, it would be $63,829; at the end of 30 years, it would be $159,972! That's pretty good for starting out with just $1,000!

Improved Spending Habit

Early investment instills financial discipline, a key skill for long-term financial success. When teens begin to invest, they naturally become more conscious of their spending habits. Regularly allocating funds for investment encourages a mindset that prioritizes saving over spending. This habit developed early, leads to better budgeting and spending decisions, fostering a responsible approach to personal finance that lasts a lifetime.

Smaller Investment Requirements

The beauty of starting to invest as a teen is that you don't need a large amount of money to see your investment grow. The longer investment period allows for smaller, more manageable contributions to accumulate into a significant corpus over time. This aspect makes investing more approachable and feasible for teens, who might only have a limited amount of money to spare. Consistent small investments can lead to significant growth, thanks to the extended time they have to multiply.

Room for Higher Risks

Youth is a time when one can afford to take more risks, and this holds true in the realm of investing. Young investors have the benefit of time, allowing them to recover from potential market downturns. This longer time horizon enables teens to invest in options with potentially higher returns, like stocks or equity mutual funds, which may carry more risk but also offer greater growth potential. Early investing also serves as a practical learning ground for understanding market dynamics and risk management, invaluable knowledge for future financial endeavors.

RISK VS. RETURN EXPLAINED

In the world of investing, the concepts of risk and return are two sides of the same coin, intricately linked and essential for any investor to understand. Financially, the terms 'risk' and 'return' are used to describe the potential loss or gain in any investment. Generally, the higher the risk of losing money on an investment, the higher the potential return, and vice versa.

The *return* on an investment is the money you earn or expect to earn from it. This can come in the form of interest, dividends, or an increase in the value of the investment itself. Returns are typically expressed as a percentage of the original investment amount. On the other hand, *risk* in investing refers to the possibility that the actual returns on an investment will be different than expected. This can mean either earning less than expected or losing some or all the original investment. The likelihood of an investment losing value is known as its risk.

Before investing, assessing your risk tolerance is important, which is your willingness or capability to lose some or all of your original investment in exchange for certain potential gains. One way to manage risk is through diversification or spreading your investments across various types of assets, sectors, or geographical areas. This can help reduce the impact if one investment performs poorly. We'll talk more about diversification later on. But ultimately, it's important to have realistic expectations about the returns you can achieve with any kind of investment. Higher returns are usually associated with higher-risk investments. Conversely, lower-risk investments typically offer lower returns.

As a young investor, understanding the relationship between risk and return is critical for making informed investment decisions. It's about finding a balance that suits your financial goals and risk tolerance. For instance, if you're saving for a long-term goal and can tolerate some level of risk, you might consider higher-risk investments with the potential for higher returns. However, if you're saving for a short-term goal or prefer a stable investment, you might opt for lower-risk options.

Remember, all investments come with some level of risk, and it's important to do your research and understand the risks and potential returns of any investment before you commit your money.

A CLOSER LOOK INTO DIVERSIFICATION

Diversification is a key investment strategy that involves spreading your investments across various financial instruments, industries, and other categories to reduce risk. The principle behind diversification is rooted in the age-old adage, "Don't put all your eggs in one basket." In the context of investing, it means not investing all your money in a single asset or type of asset.

Benefits of Diversification

Reduced Portfolio Risk

- Diversification reduces the overall risk in your investment portfolio. By spreading your investments across various assets, industries, and geographies, you are not overly exposed to the performance of a single investment. If one investment or sector underperforms, the impact on your overall portfolio is cushioned by the others that may perform better.

- Markets are unpredictable, and sectors can react differently to economic changes. Diversification helps in mitigating the impact of market volatility on your portfolio.

Enhanced Risk-Adjustment Return

- Diversification aims to reduce risk and improve the return you get for the level of risk you are willing to take. A well-diversified portfolio can help in achieving more stable and potentially higher risk-adjusted returns over the long term.
- While high-risk investments can offer high returns, they can also lead to large losses. Diversification allows you to balance high-risk investments with more stable ones, potentially leading to better overall portfolio performance.

Stabilized Economic Balance Sheet

- Different sectors and asset classes can react differently to economic events. For example, while some sectors may suffer during an economic downturn, others may remain stable or even thrive. Diversification across these areas can create an economic balance, making your portfolio more resilient to economic shifts.
- A diversified portfolio can adapt more easily to changes in the economic landscape, helping to protect your investments from sector-specific downturns.

Increased Exposure

- Diversification enables you to have a stake in various sectors and asset classes, widening your exposure to different market opportunities. This exposure can be particularly beneficial in capturing growth in emerging sectors or markets.

- For young investors, diversification provides a broader exposure to the financial markets, offering valuable learning experiences. It allows you to understand how different types of investments behave and contribute to your portfolio's performance.

Diversification Strategies

Diversification in investing is a dynamic concept with no one-size-fits-all formula. Successful investing requires a tailored approach, considering individual financial goals, risk tolerance, and time horizons. Let's take a look at different strategies to consider:

Stocks and Bonds

A fundamental diversification strategy involves a mix of stocks and bonds in your portfolio. Stocks, representing equity investments, offer the potential for higher returns but come with increased market volatility. They are suitable for growth-oriented investment strategies. On the other hand, bonds are debt investments that typically offer lower returns but provide greater stability and regular income. The balance between stocks and bonds should be aligned with your risk tolerance, investment goals, and time horizon. Younger investors often have a higher allocation towards stocks due to a longer time horizon and a higher capacity to absorb risk, while older investors might lean towards bonds for stability as they approach retirement.

Across Industries and Sectors

Investing across various industries and sectors is a strategy to protect your portfolio from fluctuations confined to a single sector. Different sectors, such as technology, healthcare, consumer goods, and energy, respond differently to economic changes. For instance, in the event of a global pandemic, consumer staples might perform better than luxury goods. By diversifying your investments across various sectors, you can mitigate the risk of significant losses if one sector underperforms.

Across Borders

Global diversification involves spreading your investments across various geographical regions. This strategy can reduce the risk associated with investing in a single country or region. Different economies may experience growth or recession at different times, so investing internationally can offer exposure to faster-growing markets and provide a buffer against local economic downturns. This can also include instances wherein certain areas of the world might be engaged in war or some kind of economy-altering situation. This strategy has the added benefit of allowing investors to benefit from emerging markets' growth potential while relying on the stability of developed markets.

Across Asset Classes

Diversification across different asset classes involves spreading investments beyond just stocks and bonds. This can include real estate, commodities like gold and oil, and even alternative investments such as hedge funds or private equity. Each asset class has its unique risk and return profile, and their performance is not always correlated. This uncorrelated performance can help in reducing the overall risk of the portfolio. For example, commodities like gold often perform well when stock markets are volatile, providing a hedge against inflation.

Across Time Frames

Also known as time diversification, this strategy involves spreading out your investment contributions over time, a technique known as dollar-cost averaging. Instead of investing a lump sum at once, you invest smaller, regular amounts at different times. This approach reduces the risk of investing a large amount at an unfavorable market price and can average out the cost of your investments over time. Regular investing, regardless of market conditions, also instills discipline and reduces the emotional impact of market fluctuations on investment decisions.

TYPES OF INVESTMENTS FOR TEENS

There are many different types of investment vehicles on the market that are supposedly designed to help your money grow. Each type of investment comes with its own level of risk and potential return. However, part of being a responsible investor is learning how these different vehicles function and the risks they entail. Here are some of the most common investment options that you might want to look into:

Mutual Funds

Mutual funds are investment vehicles that pool money from many investors to purchase a diversified portfolio of stocks, bonds, or other securities. Often managed by professional fund managers, these funds offer diversified exposure, which can help reduce risk. The risk level varies based on the fund's specific investments but is generally considered moderate. Mutual funds are an excellent choice for teens who want exposure to the stock or bond markets without the responsibility of picking individual stocks or bonds.

Exchange-Traded Fund

ETFs are similar to mutual funds but are traded on stock exchanges. They can track a wide range of assets, from market indexes to specific sectors or commodities. ETFs offer the flexibility of trading like stocks and come in a variety of risk profiles, depending on what they track. They are suitable for teens looking for diversification and the ability to conveniently buy and sell shares.

Index Fund

Index funds are a type of mutual fund or ETF designed to mirror the performance of a specific market index, like the S&P 500. These funds offer broad market exposure and are favored for their low fees and passive management style. The risk is similar to that of the market index it tracks, usually moderate to high. Index funds are a good choice for teens interested in long-term investing with broad market participation.

Stocks

Investing in stocks means buying shares in individual companies. Imagine saying that you own shares in a company like Apple or Coca-Cola! That's exactly what stock investing would be able to offer you. As a shareholder, you can benefit from the company's growth through appreciation in stock value and dividends. Stocks are known for their potential for high returns, but they also come with higher volatility and risk. Stock investing is suitable for teens with a longer investment horizon and a higher tolerance for risk.

Bonds

Bonds are debt securities where the investor loans money to a corporation or government. In return, the issuer agrees to pay interest on the investment over a set period and repay the principal at the bond's maturity. Bonds are generally lower-risk compared to stocks and offer regular income, making them a good option for teens seeking more stable, fixed-income investments.

Certificate of Deposit

We've already discussed this briefly in a previous chapter, but a Certificate of Deposit (CD) is a fixed-term deposit offered by banks. CDs provide a guaranteed interest rate over a specified term, after which the invested capital is returned. They are low-risk investments since they offer predictable returns and are often insured. CDs are ideal for teens with short-term financial goals and those looking for risk-free returns.

Savings Account

A savings account is a basic banking service that offers a safe place to store cash while earning modest interest. These accounts are very low-risk and provide easy access to funds, making them suitable for teens who need a secure place to keep their savings with some interest income. However, it's worth noting that savings accounts don't typically offer a higher yield when compared to other investment options.

IRA

An IRA is a tax-advantaged retirement savings account. There are different types of IRAs, either a traditional or a Roth, each offering specific tax benefits. Typically, young investors are recommended to start out with a Roth IRA. The investments within an IRA can vary, and so does the associated risk. IRAs are a great tool for teens to start saving for retirement early, capitalizing on the benefits of compound interest and tax savings.

If you want to get started with any of these types of investments, you'll first have to open up an account with a brokerage. Some good ones to check out are Vanguard (vanguard.com) or Fidelity (fidelity.com).

PATIENCE IS A VIRTUE

Investing is not just about choosing the right assets; it's equally about cultivating the right mindset. Patience is a critical virtue in the world of investing, especially for young investors. It's the ability to stay committed to your long-term financial goals, even in the face of market volatility and short-term fluctuations.

Stick to Longer-Term Commitments

Committing to a long-term investment strategy is essential for reaping substantial benefits. Investments typically flourish over an extended period, so it's essential to resist the urge to make abrupt decisions based on short-term market fluctuations. Historically, despite short-term volatility, markets have shown a general upward trend over long periods.

Be Consistent

Consistency in investing, often through a strategy like dollar-cost averaging, is key to building wealth over time. This approach involves regularly investing a fixed amount of money, regardless of market conditions. Such a disciplined strategy helps you avoid the pitfalls of trying to time the market, which is often unpredictable and can lead to impulsive, impatient decisions. Consistent investing not only reinforces a habit of discipline but also mitigates the risk associated with market volatility.

Invest With the Mind, Not the Heart

Investing should be guided by rational decision-making, not emotional reactions. Emotional responses to market highs and lows can lead to impulsive buying or selling, which is often detrimental to your investment goals. Instead, base your investment decisions on thorough research, a clear understanding of your financial objectives, and your personal risk tolerance.

Balance Your Portfolio's Risk Profile

A balanced risk profile is integral to maintaining patience. Regularly assess and adjust your portfolio to ensure it aligns with your current financial goals and risk appetite. This rebalancing is not about reacting to every market change but about maintaining a portfolio that reflects your evolving financial situation and goals. A well-balanced portfolio can provide peace of mind and stability, which are crucial for nurturing patience in your investment strategy.

Maintain Diversification Strategies

Diversification is a powerful tool for managing risk and instilling patience. When you spread your investments across various asset classes, sectors, and geographies, you reduce the risk of significant losses from any single investment. This diversified approach can lead to more stable and steady growth, helping you remain patient and confident in your investment strategy. Understanding the benefits of diversification can help you appreciate the gradual but more secure growth it offers, reinforcing a patient mindset.

STOCK MARKET INVESTMENT GAME

To conclude this chapter, you can test your investing prowess with an interactive game. Through this investment challenge, you will be forced to thoroughly think about the basics of how the stock market works, what factors influence stock prices, and the risks involved in investing. You can choose to play this game on your own, but it would even be more fun with friends! Here's how you can play:

Create a Fictional Investment Portfolio:

1. Each player starts with a fictional sum of money, say $10,000.
2. Players choose a few companies from different industries to invest in. For simplicity, this can be based on real companies or fictional ones
3. Allocate the fictional money to these stocks in the way you see fit.

Research Phase:

1. Players research their chosen companies. List factors that could potentially affect the stock prices of these companies (e.g., economic changes, industry news, company earnings reports).
2. Write down predictions on which way the stock price might move based on this research.

Scenario Challenges:

1. Create a series of hypothetical scenarios that could affect the stock market (e.g., an economic downturn, a global pandemic, a technological breakthrough by one of the companies, changes in government policies affecting certain industries, etc.).
2. Players decide how these scenarios would affect their portfolio and make investment decisions accordingly (buy more, sell, hold).

Question and Answer Rounds:

1. Throughout the game, introduce question rounds. Ask questions like: "What causes stock prices to rise or fall?" "What are the risks of investing in the stock market?" Players write down their answers.
2. Discuss the answers to ensure a clear understanding of the concepts.

Reflection and Learning:

1. At the end of the game, players review the performance of their portfolios based on the scenarios and decisions they made.
2. Discuss what strategies worked, what didn't, and why. Reflect on the importance of research and understanding market risks.

Game Conclusion:

1. The winner can be determined by who made the most profit in their portfolio or who best understood and managed the risks.
2. Conclude with a discussion on what was learned about the stock market, the importance of research, and risk management in investing.

If you're a complete beginner and you're just starting out in this world, use simple scenarios that are familiar to you and focus on more basic investing concepts. The more advanced you become, the more you can start to introduce complex scenarios and explore strategies like diversification and long-term versus short-term investing. The point of this game isn't necessarily to win. Rather, it's to help you develop an understanding of how to structure your investment strategy based on information that is provided to you.

In the next chapter, we're going to shift gears once more and talk about a concept that often gets unfairly demonized in the world of finance: debt. More specifically, we'll be talking all about credit, what it is, and how it fits into the world of personal finance.

CHAPTER 9
GET CREDIT WISE

If you don't take good care of your credit, then your credit won't take good care of you.

TYLER GREGORY

DEBT, credit, borrowing money. You don't necessarily have to fear these things when it comes to your personal finance journey. In fact, you can make these things work to your advantage as long as you know all the strategies involved in doing so. The truth is that credit can be a powerful tool if used wisely. It can help you achieve major financial goals, like buying a car or financing your education. However, mismanagement of credit can lead to debt that hampers your financial well-being. Thus, mastering the fundamentals of credit is indispensable.

CREDIT CARDS EXPLAINED

In the previous section, you might have noticed the emphasis on the proper usage of credit cards. Now, it's possible that you have a tainted view of credit cards because of horror stories that you may have heard about people falling into very bad credit card debt. While it's true that many people use credit cards irresponsibly, that doesn't mean that credit cards can't be used as effective financial tools.

What Are Credit Cards, and How Do They Work?

Credit cards are financial instruments issued by banks or financial institutions, allowing you to borrow funds up to a certain limit for purchases or cash withdrawals. Unlike debit cards, which use funds you already have in your bank account, credit cards provide access to a line of credit. This means you are borrowing money that must be paid back, typically with interest, if not paid within a specific period. Credit cards also have various features and benefits, such as reward points, cashback, travel perks, etc. They are a form of unsecured loan, as they don't require any collateral.

When you use a credit card, the card issuer pays the merchant on your behalf, reducing your available credit by the amount of the purchase. You are then obligated to pay back this amount to the card issuer. Credit cards operate on a billing cycle, usually monthly. At the end of each cycle, the issuer sends a statement detailing all transactions, the total amount owed (statement balance), the minimum payment due, and the payment due date.

If you pay the statement balance in full by the due date, you usually won't be charged interest (thanks to the grace period). However, if you only make the minimum payment or partial payment, the remaining balance will carry over to the next billing cycle and accrue interest. Also, each credit card comes with a credit limit, which is the maximum amount you can borrow. Exceeding this limit can result in fees and negatively impact your credit score.

How Are Credit Cards Used?

- **Card Purchases:** The most common use of credit cards is for everyday purchases, like shopping, dining, and online transactions. They offer a convenient and secure payment method without the need for cash.
- **Bank Transfers:** Some credit cards allow you to transfer part of your credit limit as cash into your bank account. This can be useful in emergencies but usually incurs a higher interest rate and fees, so it's best to avoid using a credit card for this purpose.

- **Money Transfers:** Credit cards can also be used for transferring money to other individuals, though this also often comes with fees and immediate interest charges. Again, it's best to avoid money transfers.
- **Cash Advances:** You can use credit cards to withdraw cash from ATMs, known as a cash advance. However, cash advances typically attract high-interest rates from the day of the transaction, along with cash advance fees. And cash advances are also best to be avoided, unless for a real emergency.

Pros and Cons of Owning a Credit Card

One of the main goals of this entire section is to enlighten you on how it's possible to have a good relationship with credit and how you can even capitalize on credit to improve your financial standing. However, there's a reason why credit cards get such a bad rap in mainstream dialogue. The truth is that credit cards are a double-edged sword in personal finance, offering both advantages and potential pitfalls. It's important that you take the time to thoroughly understand the pros and cons of owning a credit card just so you're aware of all the risks and benefits involved.

Pros:

- **Building Credit History:** Regular use of a credit card and timely payments can help build a positive credit history, which is essential for future financial activities like securing a loan or renting an apartment.
- **Convenience:** Credit cards offer a convenient way to pay for in-person and online purchases. They eliminate the need to carry large amounts of cash and can be particularly useful in emergencies or unexpected expenses.
- **Rewards and Benefits:** Many credit cards offer rewards such as cashback, airline miles, or points that can be redeemed for goods and services. These rewards can provide significant value if the card is used wisely.
- **Global Acceptance:** Credit cards are widely accepted around the world, making them a convenient option for international

travel and purchases.

Cons:

- **Risk of Debt:** The ease of using credit cards can lead to overspending and accumulating debt. Interest charges on unpaid balances can compound quickly, making it difficult to pay off the debt.
- **High-Interest Rates:** Credit cards generally have higher interest rates compared to other forms of credit. If balances are not paid in full each month, the interest can significantly increase the total amount owed.
- **Impact on Credit Score:** Mismanagement of a credit card, such as late payments or maxing out your credit limit, can negatively impact your credit score.
- **Fees and Penalties:** Credit cards can come with various fees, including annual fees, late payment fees, and charges for transactions like cash advances and foreign transactions.
- **Potential for Fraud:** While credit cards offer fraud protection, they can still be susceptible to theft and fraudulent activities. It requires vigilance in monitoring account statements and safeguarding card information.

Again, owning a credit card does have its fair share of benefits. But part of being a responsible credit card owner and user means also being aware of the potential cons. Ultimately, as long as you stay disciplined in your practice as a credit card owner, there's no reason why it shouldn't be able to serve you well throughout your life.

Credit Cards for Teens

So, you might be convinced that you want a credit card for yourself. Should you just walk into a bank and get one? Unfortunately, it's not as simple as that. Being a teenager does have its limits when it comes to getting a credit card of your own. Given that you're still underage, there are specific considerations and options regarding credit card usage that you should know about. Here are some of the options that you might want to consider:

Supplementary Cards From Parents' Accounts

A common way for teens to gain credit card experience is by becoming an authorized user on a parent's account. This arrangement lets you own a card linked to your parents' credit accounts. As an authorized user, you can start building a credit history, which is beneficial for future financial endeavors. However, this method requires a high level of responsibility and trust. Your parent remains ultimately responsible for the account, and your spending habits directly impact your parent's credit. Therefore, clear communication about spending habits and limits is essential in this arrangement.

Co-Signing Credit Cards

For teens under 18, obtaining a co-signed credit card is another option. In this case, a parent or guardian co-signs the credit card application, agreeing to take joint responsibility for the account. The activity on this card will affect both your and the co-signer's credit scores. This shared responsibility means that both parties need to be vigilant about how the card is used, ensuring payments are made on time, and spending is kept under control.

Getting Parents' or Guardians' Support or Approval

Before you start thinking about getting your own credit card, it's important to have a conversation with your parents or guardians. Talk about why you want a credit card, how you plan to use it, and how you'll handle the responsibility that comes with it. This is a great chance for you to learn from their experiences and for them to guide you on the path to financial savvy.

Choosing the Right Card

There are too many variables that go into the decision of choosing your very first credit card. But this is all a part of the excitement of being a first-time credit card owner. Fortunately, there's no shortage of options for you out there right now. Many banks and financial institutions offer their own versions of teen-friendly credit cards. Here are some that you might want to consider:

- **Capital One Platinum Secured Credit Card:** This card is designed for individuals looking to build or rebuild their credit. As a secured card, it requires a refundable security deposit, which becomes your credit limit. It's an excellent choice if you're starting from scratch with your credit history.

- **Petal 2 Visa Credit Card:** The Petal 2 is a unique card that doesn't necessarily require a credit history for approval. It uses alternative data like your banking history to determine creditworthiness, which is great if you're new to credit. It offers cashback rewards on eligible purchases and doesn't charge any fees, not even late payment fees, which is rare for a credit card.
- **Bank of America Customized Cash Rewards Secured Credit Card:** This secured card allows you to earn cashback while building your credit. It requires a security deposit but offers rewards in return, making it a good option if you can handle the responsibility of a rewards card.
- **JetBlue Plus Card:** For teens who travel frequently, especially on JetBlue, this card offers valuable travel rewards. It's a good fit if you're already a bit credit-savvy and travel enough to offset the annual fee with rewards.

Now, keep in mind that all the information presented here may not be accurate or up-to-date during the time that you're reading it. It's always best to do your own research before coming to a decision.

How to Use Your Credit Cards Responsibly to Build Credit

The prospect of getting a credit card might signify a shift into financial independence on your end, and that's certainly true! However, these credit cards aren't just privileges; they're also your responsibility. Using a credit card wisely is pivotal for building a good credit score, which can impact many aspects of your future financial life. Let's dive into how you can use credit cards responsibly to build and maintain good credit.

Pay Attention to Interest

When you use a credit card, you're borrowing money that needs to be paid back. If you don't pay the full balance by the due date, interest charges accrue on the remaining amount. This interest can add up quickly and increase the total amount you owe. Understanding how interest works and the rates your card charges is crucial. Try to pay off your balance in full each month to avoid these charges.

Don't Get Too Many Credit Cards

It might be tempting to sign up for several credit cards, especially with various rewards programs and signup bonuses out there. However, having too many can make it harder to manage your finances and keep track of spending. Each new card also results in a hard inquiry on your credit report, which can temporarily lower your score. Stick to one or two cards, especially when you're just starting.

Watch Out for Debt Settlement Scams

Be cautious of companies that claim they can fix your credit for a fee or settle your debt for less than what you owe. Many of these are scams.

Pay Credit Card Bills on Time

One of the most important aspects of credit card use is paying your bills on time. Late payments can severely damage your credit score. Set reminders or automatic payments to ensure you never miss a due date. Even paying the minimum is better than paying late. The best practice is to make sure that you're paying your credit card build on-time and in full every single month.

Don't Spend Beyond the Limit

Your credit card comes with a spending limit, and it's important not to exceed it. Maxing out your credit card can hurt your credit score, as it increases your credit utilization ratio.

Monitor Monthly Statements

Regularly check your credit card statements for errors or unauthorized transactions. This helps in managing your spending and also protects against potential fraud or billing mistakes. Promptly report any discrepancies to your credit card issuer.

Keep the Balance Low

A low balance relative to your credit limit is good for your credit score. High balances can indicate over-reliance on credit and risk to lenders.

Aim to use less than 30% of your available credit and pay off your balances regularly to keep your credit utilization low.

BUILDING CREDIT

In the realm of personal finance, credit refers to your ability to borrow money with the promise to repay it later, typically with interest. It's a fundamental component of modern financial systems, allowing for the purchase of goods or services without immediate payment. Having good credit means that you are considered trustworthy by lenders and financial institutions based on your history of managing borrowed money. It signifies that you have a history of responsibly managing debt and making timely payments. Also, good credit reflects a positive impression of your financial behavior, suggesting that you are a low-risk borrower.

Understanding Credit Scores

A credit score is a numerical representation of your creditworthiness. Think of it as a grading system for how well you pay back your debts. It's calculated based on your credit history, which includes factors like your payment history, the amount of debt you have, the length of your credit history, the types of credit you use, and recent credit inquiries. Lenders use credit scores to assess the risk of lending to you. Typically, these scores range from 300 to 850. The higher your score, the better your creditworthiness. Generally, a score of 670 and above is considered good (Gravier, 2023). A higher score indicates to lenders that you're a trustworthy borrower, which can lead to better interest rates and loan terms.

The Benefits of Having a Good Credit Score

Of course, it goes without saying that you should always strive to have a good credit score. But let's explore even further why having such a goal would be good for you in the long run:

- **Easier Credit Approval:** A good credit score opens the door to easier approval for credit cards and loans. Lenders view a good credit score as an indication of financial responsibility and reliability.

- **Lower Interest Rates:** One of the most tangible benefits of a good credit score is qualifying for lower interest rates on loans and credit cards. Lower rates mean you'll pay less over the life of a loan, which can save you significant amounts of money, especially on large, long-term loans like mortgages.
- **Better Loan Terms:** A good credit score can lead to more favorable terms on loans, such as higher borrowing limits and more flexible repayment options. You have better negotiating power to discuss terms with lenders, potentially leading to more customized and beneficial loan arrangements.
- **Lower Insurance Premiums:** Many car insurance companies use credit scores as part of determining your insurance rates. A good credit score can translate into lower premiums, as insurers often consider those with higher credit scores as lower risk.
- **Easier Car/Home Purchases:** When the time comes to purchase a car or even a home, a good credit score simplifies the process. It not only increases the likelihood of loan approval but also may afford you a wider range of choices due to higher credit limits.

The Keys to Building and Maintaining Good Credit Scores

Maintaining a good credit score might seem like a daunting task, especially as a young teen with an infantile understanding of personal finance. But you might take solace in the fact that only around 16% of Americans have *bad credit* (Ulzheimer, 2023). That means that a vast majority of people tend to be fairly good at maintaining decent credit scores! With the right approach and habits, managing your credit scores is a lot easier than you think.

Starting With a Beginner's Credit Card or Secured Credit Card

For those new to credit, beginning with a credit card designed for beginners or a secured credit card is a wise move. These cards are tailored for individuals without a credit history and can be an excellent starting point for building credit. The key is to use these cards judiciously. Make small purchases that you can afford to pay off each month and ensure that you pay the full balance on time. This practice helps establish a pattern of responsible credit use and timely payments.

The Importance of Timely Payments

The most important factor in your credit score is your payment history. Consistently paying your credit card bill on time each month cannot be overstressed. Even one late payment can negatively impact your credit score. To avoid missing payments, you can set up reminders or automate your payments. This consistent, on-time payment behavior will positively influence your credit score over time.

Keeping Credit Utilization Low

Credit utilization (how much of your available credit you're using) is another critical factor in determining your credit score. It's recommended to keep your credit utilization below 30% of your credit limit. High utilization can indicate potential over-reliance on credit, which can be a red flag to lenders. Monitoring your credit card usage and keeping spending in check are essential to maintaining a healthy credit score.

Being Mindful of Credit Applications

Every time you apply for new credit, it results in a hard inquiry into your credit report, which can slightly lower your credit score. Applying for several credit lines in a short period can accumulate these negative impacts. Hence, it's important to be thoughtful and selective when applying for new credit. It's better to build your credit history gradually rather than rushing into multiple credit agreements.

Monitoring Your Credit Report

Regularly monitoring your credit report is an important habit. It helps you stay informed about your credit status and allows you to check for any inaccuracies or signs of fraudulent activity. You can access free credit reports from various sources, such as the three main credit bureaus, Experian, TransUnion and Equifax. Regularly reviewing these reports can help you maintain a good credit score.

Diversifying Credit Types

Having a mix of different types of credit can positively affect your credit score. This diversity shows lenders that you can handle various types of credit responsibly. However, it's important to avoid taking on unnecessary debt. New credit should only be pursued when it aligns with your financial needs and goals.

Avoid Closing Old Credit Cards

The length of your credit history contributes to your credit score. Keeping older credit card accounts open, even if you don't use them frequently, helps to extend your credit history, which can be beneficial for your score. Just make sure these accounts don't carry high balances and are kept in good standing.

DEBT MANAGEMENT

Debt and credit. What's the difference? Well, even though these two concepts are closely related, they aren't entirely the same. Credit refers to your ability to borrow money or access financial goods and services with the understanding that you'll eventually pay it off. It's essentially a measure of trust that lenders and creditors have in you. Debt, on the other hand, is what you incur when you use credit; it's the actual amount you owe. Having access to credit doesn't automatically mean you're in debt; it only becomes debt once you borrow and have an obligation to repay.

Debt can come in all sorts of shapes and sizes:

- **Secured Debt:** This type of debt is backed by collateral, an asset that the lender can take if you fail to repay the loan. Examples include mortgages (secured by your home) and auto loans (secured by your vehicle). The presence of collateral generally means lower interest rates, as the lender has a safety net.
- **Unsecured Debt:** Unsecured debt doesn't involve any collateral. Credit cards and most personal loans fall into this category. Because there's more risk for the lender, interest rates for unsecured debts are usually higher.

- **Revolving Debt:** This is a form of credit that can be repeatedly used up to a certain limit as long as the account is open and payments are made on time. Credit cards are the most common type of revolving debt. They allow you to borrow repeatedly up to your credit limit without applying for a new loan each time.
- **Credit Cards:** While they fall under revolving debt, credit cards deserve a special mention. They're a common form of unsecured debt and can have high-interest rates, especially if balances are carried over from month to month.
- **Mortgages:** These are loans specifically used to purchase real estate. Mortgages are typically long-term loans, with repayment periods often extending up to 30 years.
- **Student Loans:** These loans are designed to help students pay for education-related expenses. They can be federal or private, with varying terms and conditions.
- **Auto Loans:** These loans are used to purchase vehicles. Similar to mortgages, auto loans are secured by the asset purchased— in this case, the vehicle.

Bad Debt vs. Good Debt

Now, debt is bad, right? Well, not necessarily. Did you know that some of the richest and most successful people in the world have debts? You would be surprised at how many times the wealthy make use of debt to build on their wealth. That's because debt isn't always bad. In fact, in many cases, it can be used for good. Let's take a look at the differences:

Good debt can be thought of as an investment that will grow in value or generate long-term income. Taking on this kind of debt can be beneficial if it leads to financial growth or adds significant value to your life. Examples of good debt can include:

- **Educational Loans:** Taking a student loan to pay for college can be considered good debt. Education is an investment in your future earning potential. A college degree often leads to better job prospects and higher income over your lifetime.

- **Mortgages:** If you buy a home with a mortgage, this can also be good debt. Real estate typically appreciates in value over time, and owning a home can be a key part of building wealth.
- **Business Loans:** Borrowing money to start a business or fund a startup can be risky, but if the business succeeds, it can significantly increase your earning potential.

On the other hand, bad debt typically involves borrowing money for purchases that quickly lose value and do not generate long-term income. Bad debt often comes with high interest rates and can lead to a cycle of debt if not managed carefully. Here are examples of bad debt:

- **Credit Card Debt for Non-Essentials:** Using a credit card to buy the latest phone, designer clothes, or other luxury items that you can't afford to pay off immediately can be considered bad debt. These items depreciate quickly, and if you carry a balance, the high interest can make the cost of these items even higher.
- **High-Interest Auto Loans for Expensive Cars:** While an auto loan can be necessary to buy a vehicle, choosing a high-end car that stretches your budget can lead to burdensome debt. Cars typically depreciate in value quickly, and if the loan has a high-interest rate, you might end up owing more than the car is worth.
- **Payday Loans:** These are short-term, high-interest loans that are often used to cover expenses until your next paycheck. They can be extremely costly due to high fees and interest rates, making them a form of bad debt.

As you can see, debt isn't inherently good or bad. It all depends on how you use that money to serve your financial goals and lifestyle.

Strategies to Manage Debt Effectively

As you've learned, debt, when used properly, can be a powerful tool in achieving financial goals. However, it's a common pitfall to fall into a debt trap, which can significantly hinder your financial standing and future opportunities. Fortunately, there are ways you can manage debt effectively so that you never end up being enslaved by it:

- **Only Use Debt for Needs, Not Wants:** Before taking on debt, it's important to differentiate between needs and wants. Needs are essential expenses like education, a reliable vehicle, or a mortgage. Wants are non-essential and often include luxury items or discretionary spending.
- **If You Can't Afford It, Don't Use a Credit Card to Buy It:** A fundamental rule of personal finance is to live within your means. If you can't afford to pay cash for a non-essential item, you shouldn't put it on your credit card.
- **Have an Emergency Fund to Fall Back On:** An emergency fund is a savings account set aside to cover unexpected expenses, like medical emergencies or car repairs. Having this fund can prevent you from needing to rely on high-interest credit cards or loans in times of need.
- **Have a Debt Payment Plan in Place:** Develop a plan to pay off your debts. This might involve strategies like the debt snowball method (paying off smaller debts first for psychological wins) or the debt avalanche method (focusing on debts with the highest interest rates first). We'll explore these strategies in-depth after this section.

Again, accruing debt isn't bad as long as you pay your bills on time. You just have to ensure that you have the proper headspace and strategy in place that will allow you to never fall into the trap of always being in debt.

Debt Repayment Strategies

Realistically speaking, as a teen, you shouldn't be worrying about finding yourself in debt this early in life. However, once you get into college and enter adulthood, you will be surprised at how easily it can be to accrue debt, especially when you're not paying attention. Ideally, you must manage your finances to minimize debt (especially bad debt) as much as possible. However, if you find yourself in a position wherein you have to start paying off a substantial amount of debt, it's important to approach this task systematically and methodically. Here are a few common strategies you might want to consider:

Debt Snowball Method:

- The debt snowball method involves paying off your debts, starting with the smallest balance first while maintaining minimum payments on all other debts. Once the smallest debt is paid off, you move on to the next smallest, and so on.
- This method can be motivating because you see results quickly. Each debt you pay off gives you a confidence boost and motivation to tackle the next one.

Debt Avalanche Method:

- The debt avalanche method prioritizes paying off debts with the highest interest rates first while making minimum payments on the rest. After the highest-interest debt is cleared, you move on to the one with the next highest interest rate.
- This method can save you money on interest payments over time and is generally the faster way to reduce your overall debt, even though it might take longer to pay off the first debt.

Debt Consolidation:

- Debt consolidation involves combining multiple debts into a single loan with a lower interest rate. This can simplify your payments, as you only have to worry about one payment instead of multiple.
- Often, the consolidated loan has a lower interest rate, which can reduce the amount you pay over time and help you pay off your debt faster.

Again, it's rare for teens to find themselves in significant debt, but it's not unheard of, especially with the availability of student loans and credit cards. If you do find yourself in debt, these strategies can help you manage and eventually eliminate that debt in a systematic manner.

ARE YOU READY FOR A CREDIT CARD?

Even though we spent a substantial amount of time talking about them, the truth is that credit cards are not necessities in personal finance, particularly for teens. While they can be useful tools for building credit and convenient for making purchases, they also come with significant responsibilities. Deciding to get a credit card should not be taken lightly. It's necessary to assess whether you're truly ready for the responsibility that comes with having a credit card. To help you determine your readiness, I've prepared a list of questions. Take some time to answer these questions honestly in your journal. Your responses will help you gauge whether you're prepared for the responsibilities of having a credit card.

- *Why do I want a credit card?*
- *Can I reliably pay off credit card bills each month?*
- *Am I good at budgeting?*
- *How do I handle my current financial responsibilities?*
- *Do I understand how interest and credit card fees work?*
- *Am I aware of the consequences of not paying the full balance each month?*
- *Am I aware of how credit card usage can affect my credit score and future financial opportunities?*
- *Have I researched different types of credit cards?*
- *Do I know what kind of credit card I want for myself?*

These questions provide you with an opportunity for reflection. Again, a credit card isn't necessary and it's okay that you don't have one just yet. But, upon thorough reflection, if you realize that you're ready for a credit card, there should be no problem initiating the steps to acquire one.

This is just one of the many important decisions you will have to make about your finances. It's essential to reiterate the point that these decisions will have a profound impact on your future, which brings us to the topic of the next chapter: planning for the long game.

CHAPTER 10
PLAN FOR THE LONG GAME

Planning is bringing the future into the present so that you can do something about it now.

ALAN LAKEIN

THE FINAL CHAPTER! Congratulations! What an amazing journey you've had so far. Seriously, just think about it. Reflect on the kind of person that you were before you started reading this book, and think about all of the knowledge and information that you've gained along the way. Your growth is substantial and should not be taken for granted. However, in the grand scheme of things, we've only just begun. You're at a pivotal point in your life where the decisions you make can significantly shape your financial journey ahead. Long-term financial planning and goal setting might seem like concepts far off in the future, but starting early can set you on a path to incredible success. In this chapter, we're going to peer into our crystal balls and take a deep look into your bright future and all the steps you need to take to get there.

FINANCIAL PLANNING EXPLAINED

The older you get, the more you're going to hear about the concept of *financial planning*. Now, it's important that you understand what that means so that you don't get any wrong notions of what it is in the future. A financial plan is essentially a roadmap for your money. It's a comprehensive overview of your current financial situation, your financial goals, and the strategies you'll use to achieve those goals. Think of it as a personalized guide that helps you manage your income, expenses, savings, and investments for now and the future.

Having a financial plan gives you a clear direction. It helps you understand where you are financially and what you need to do to get where you want to be. Specifically, financial plans help you to achieve your goals that require money or funding. Whether your goal is to save for college, buy a car, or start a small business, a financial plan can help you set and achieve these goals in a structured way. Ultimately, a sound financial plan leads to financial security. As they say, failing to plan is planning to fail. Having a solid financial plan in place sets you up for success.

Short-Term Goals

Short-term goals are objectives you aim to achieve within a relatively brief period, typically within a year or two. Examples could include saving for a new phone, buying a concert ticket, or funding a summer vacation. For short-term goals, your financial plan might focus on budgeting and saving strategies. It involves setting aside a certain amount of money regularly, perhaps from a part-time job or allowance, and strictly managing your expenses to ensure you reach your savings target within the desired timeframe.

Medium-Term Goals

Medium-term goals are those you plan to accomplish in the next two to five years. These might include saving for a car, funding a significant trip, or starting a college savings fund. Achieving medium-term goals often requires a more disciplined approach. Your financial plan here may include a mix of regular savings and perhaps some low-risk investments. It's also about balancing these goals with your short-term needs, ensuring that saving for these goals doesn't hinder your current financial stability.

Long-Term Goals

Long-term goals are the ones you aim to achieve over a longer period, often five years or more into the future. Examples include saving for a down payment on a house, planning for higher education, or even beginning to build a retirement fund. They require a more complex financial strategy, often involving a diversified investment portfolio. Since these goals have a longer time horizon, your financial plan can afford to incorporate investments that carry more risk but offer higher returns, like stocks or mutual funds.

BUYING YOUR FIRST CAR

For many teens like you, owning a car is more than just a purchase; it's a rite of passage. It symbolizes freedom and independence. Imagine finally being able to go where you want, when you want. The excitement of choosing your first car, the thrill of taking the driver's seat, and the sense of ownership are unparalleled experiences. However, the decision to buy a car involves much more than just the vehicle itself. It's a significant financial commitment that extends beyond the initial purchase price. So, just because you think you have enough money saved up to pay for the number of a car's price tag, think again.

When you're planning to buy your first car, it's important to consider all the costs associated with car ownership. Let's break down these costs so you can factor them into your financial planning:

- **Fuel:** This ongoing expense can vary depending on how much you drive, the type of car you choose, and fluctuating fuel prices. Fuel-efficient cars can save you money in the long run, so consider fuel economy when selecting your vehicle.
- **Insurance:** Auto insurance is a must, but it can be quite costly, especially for teen drivers. Insurance rates depend on various factors, including the type of car, your driving record, and even your grades. Shop around for the best insurance rates and consider whether you'll be on your parent's policy or if you need your own.
- **Maintenance and Repairs:** Regular maintenance is critical to keep your car running smoothly and can prevent costly repairs

down the line—budget for routine services like oil changes, tire rotations, and brake checks. Also, set aside some money for unexpected repairs—cars can be unpredictable.

- **Registration Fees and Taxes:** When you buy a car, you'll need to pay for registration and possibly state taxes. These fees vary by state and vehicle type, so check your local requirements.
- **Depreciation:** Cars lose value over time, a cost known as depreciation. New cars depreciate quickly in the first few years, which is something to consider if you're looking at brand-new models. Used cars might offer more value since they've already undergone significant depreciation.

Owning a car is a big responsibility and requires careful financial planning. Buying a car is expensive, but *owning* a car and actually maintaining it can be even *more* expensive.

How to Pay for Your First Car

When it comes to actually purchasing your first car, there are several approaches you can take, each with its own set of benefits and drawbacks. It's important to consider your financial situation, how long you plan to keep the car, and what you can afford in terms of monthly payments and upfront costs. Let's explore the three common vehicle payment methods: buying outright, getting a loan, and leasing.

- **Buying It Outright:** Buying a car outright involves paying the full purchase price in cash. This means no monthly payments or interest charges. The biggest advantage is that you own the car completely and don't have to worry about monthly payments. You also avoid interest charges that come with loans. Additionally, owning the car means you have the freedom to sell it at any time.
- **Getting a Loan:** Taking out a loan means borrowing money from a bank, credit union, or other lender to pay for the car. You then pay back this amount, plus interest, over a set period. That means you don't need to cough up the cash upfront to purchase a car. The downside is the interest. Over time, you'll end up paying more for the car than its initial price. Also, your car will depreciate, meaning it could be

worth less than what you owe at some point during the loan term.

- **Leasing:** Leasing a car is similar to renting. You make monthly payments to use the car for a fixed term (usually two to four years). At the end of the lease, you can either return the car, purchase it for a predetermined price, or start a new lease. It's a great way to use a car without committing to actually paying for one. The major drawback is that you don't own the car. You have to return it at the end of the lease unless you decide to buy it. There are also restrictions on mileage and customization, and you could face fees for excessive wear and tear. From a financial standpoint, this typically isn't the best option.

PLANNING FOR COLLEGE

Planning for college is an important step in your journey toward higher education and future career success. You've probably been lectured ad nauseam on the dramatic impact that a college education can have on your life. So, there's really no need to belabor that point any further. As you approach this significant milestone, it's crucial to understand not just the importance of a college education but also the financial implications and strategies for effectively saving for it.

A college education is often seen as a pathway to expanded career opportunities, higher earning potential, and broader knowledge and skills development. It can open doors to professions and opportunities that might otherwise be unavailable. Beyond academics, college offers a unique environment for personal growth, networking, and developing critical life skills. But it's also true that college can get really expensive, and we need to do a thorough breakdown of the finances involved in order for us to really be able to plan for it effectively.

How Much Should You Have Saved Up?

Unfortunately, there's no singular answer. The amount you should save for college depends on various factors, including the type of college (public versus private), the anticipated duration of your study (2-year, 4-year, or more), and whether you'll be living at home or on campus. Don't forget to factor in other expenses like books, supplies, and personal expenses.

The best thing you can do right now is to look into the current costs of colleges you're interested in and consider how much these costs might rise in the future. Creating a budget that covers tuition, accommodation, books, and living expenses will give you a clearer savings target. Remember what we learned about compound interest? Starting early also reduces the financial burden as you get closer to college age.

How to Start Your Own College Fund

Starting your own college fund can be done as early as now. And the best part is that the process of doing so shouldn't be any different from any other long-term saving plan that you might have:

- **Open a Dedicated Savings Account:** Consider opening a savings account specifically for college funds. Some accounts are designed for education savings, like 529 plans in the United States, which offer tax advantages for college savings.
- **Regular Contributions:** Make regular contributions to this fund. You can start with whatever amount you're comfortable with and increase it as your financial situation allows.
- **Involve Family Members:** Family members might be willing to contribute to your college fund. Let them know about your goals and how they can help.

Again, planning for your college education as early as now might seem like such a burden, but it will save you a lot of hassles down the line. Remember that college is a significant investment in your future, and thoughtful planning can make it more achievable.

Alternative Financial Options

If you're paying for your college education out of pocket, then good for you. That's a sign of humility, maturity, and industriousness on your part. However, there's no disregard for the fact that a college education can be expensive. There's no shame in exhausting all the options at your disposal for financial relief. Here are a few alternative financial relief options that you might want to look into as you're preparing for this big expense:

Scholarships and Grants

Scholarships and grants are types of financial aid that you don't have to repay. They can be based on various criteria, including academic achievement, athletic skills, community service, or special interests. Start researching scholarships and grants early. Look for opportunities from schools, private companies, nonprofits, and community groups. Apply to as many as you can. Keep in mind that even smaller awards can really add up. If you don't know where to start, your high school counselors can be a great resource for finding scholarships and grants. They often have information about local scholarships as well as national opportunities.

Work-Study Programs or Part-Time Jobs

Work-study programs provide part-time jobs for undergraduate and graduate students with financial challenges, giving them the resources to help pay education-related expenses. In the U.S., the Federal Work-Study Program, in particular, is able to offer funds for flexible employment to help students finance the costs of education. Check with your intended school's financial aid office to see if they participate in the program.

Payment Plans

Many colleges offer payment plans allowing you to pay your tuition in installments rather than in one lump sum. This can make college expenses more manageable and less overwhelming. If you do enough research, you might even find some interest-free plans, making them an attractive option compared to loans. Check with the college's financial aid or bursar's office to learn about available plans.

Again, college is a privilege, albeit a very expensive privilege. You must do everything that you can now to ease your financial burdens in the future if you know that you truly are going to pursue a college education.

MOVING OUT OF THE HOUSE AT 18

The big 18! It's the age when you officially step outside of your comfort zone and venture out into the world as a young adult. Turning 18 often brings the exciting prospect of moving out of your parent's home and starting a more independent phase of life. As you may have noticed with other milestones mentioned in this book, it's important that you practice proper financial preparation to ensure a smooth transition to this next step in your life. Here's a checklist of tasks that you might want to pay attention to:

Creating a Pre-Move Plan

- Start planning at least six months in advance. This gives you ample time to get a job if you don't already have one, start saving money, build your credit, and research where you want to live.
- Secure a steady source of income. This will be crucial for covering your living expenses once you move out. If you already have a job, consider whether your current income will support your living costs independently.
- If you haven't already, start building your credit. A good credit score will make renting an apartment, setting up utilities, and managing other financial aspects of living independently easier.

Financial Foundations

- **Bank Accounts:** If you don't have them already, open both checking and savings accounts. These will be essential for managing your finances.
- **Create a Monthly Budget:** Based on your income, draft a budget that accounts for rent, utilities, food, transportation, insurance, and any other regular expenses.
- **Emergency Savings:** Aim to save at least three to six months' worth of living expenses before moving out. This emergency fund can be a lifesaver in case of unexpected expenses or job loss.

Communication and Housing Logistics

- **Discuss with Your Family:** Communicate your plans with your family. They can offer support, advice, and perhaps even some essential items for your new place.
- **Finding Housing:** Look for housing options within your budget. Consider the cost of rent, location, and amenities. Don't forget to factor in the security deposit and any initial setup costs.
- **Setting Up Utilities:** Research and arrange for utilities like electricity, water, gas, and internet in your new place. Remember, these costs should be included in your monthly budget.

Apart from financial readiness, ensure you're equipped with basic life skills. This includes knowing how to cook, clean, do laundry, and manage other household tasks. These skills will be essential for living on your own. This book might be about personal finance, but there are other aspects of adulting that you should also be paying attention to.

SAVING FOR RETIREMENT

It might seem odd to start thinking about retirement when you're just stepping into adulthood, but in the world of personal finance, it's a smart move. Starting to plan and save for retirement at a young age can set the foundation for a secure financial future. We've already talked about compound interest and how the money you save in your teens and twenties has more time to grow, meaning you could end up with a significantly larger retirement fund.

Starting early means you can save smaller amounts regularly rather than trying to catch up later in life. This can reduce financial stress and make saving for retirement more manageable. Now, granted, other aspects of life require your immediate attention, but it's still worth looking into how you can best prepare for retirement even while you're young.

- **401(k)s:** If you have a job that offers a 401(k) plan, consider participating, especially if your employer matches contributions. This is a tax-advantaged retirement savings account where contributions are made directly from your paycheck.
- **IRAs (Individual Retirement Accounts):** An IRA is a retirement savings account that offers tax advantages. There are two main types: Traditional IRAs, where contributions may be tax-deductible, and Roth IRAs, where contributions are made with after-tax dollars but withdrawals in retirement are tax-free.
- **Roth IRAs for Teens:** Roth IRAs can be particularly advantageous for teens since you're likely in a lower tax bracket now than you will be later in life. The money in a Roth IRA grows tax-free, and you can withdraw your contributions (but not the earnings) at any time without penalty.

Ultimately, it would be best to begin by saving a small, manageable portion of any money you earn. Even if it's just a few dollars from a part-time job or allowance, these contributions can add up over time. As your income increases, gradually increase your retirement contributions. The goal is to make saving for retirement a regular habit.

VISION BOARDING

For the book's final interactive element, we're going to create a vision board together. A vision board is a great way of concretizing everything that you want to achieve. It can serve as a daily reminder of your goals and be an incredible motivator for you as you try to stay disciplined in your financial journey. On days when financial planning seems challenging, your vision board will remind you of why you're working hard and saving money.

What You'll Need:

- Corkboard/Poster Board
- Magazines/Printouts

- Markers
- Glue
- Scissors
- Other arts and crafts materials

Steps

1. Gather Your Materials: You'll need a large piece of poster board or a corkboard, magazines, printouts, markers, glue, scissors, and any other craft supplies you enjoy using.
2. Reflect on Your Goals: Think about your long-term financial goals. These could include saving for college, buying a car, traveling, owning a home, or starting to save for retirement.
3. Find Visual Representations: Look through magazines or search online for images and words that represent your goals. For example, if one of your goals is to save for college, you might include a picture of a graduation cap or the logo of the university you want to attend.
4. Be Creative: Arrange and paste your images and words on your board in a way that's visually appealing to you. You can also write down specific financial goals, motivational quotes, or milestones.
5. Place It in Your Room: Position your vision board somewhere in your room where you'll see it every day. This regular visual reminder will help keep your financial goals at the forefront of your mind.

Creating a vision board is a unique way to make the process of financial planning more tangible and engaging. It's a constant visual reminder of your financial dreams and the steps you need to take to achieve them.

KEEPING THE GAME ALIVE

Congratulations on reaching the end of this amazing journey! Now that you've loaded up on all the cool tips and tricks for achieving financial independence, you've got a superpower that others are looking for. And guess what? You can share this superpower with them!

Leaving your honest thoughts about this book on Amazon is like passing the baton in the coolest race ever. You're showing other teens where to find the golden keys to financial wisdom. Just imagine, your words could inspire someone else to start their own journey towards smart money management!

So, here's your chance to make a difference. Use the QR code below to leave a review:

By sharing your insights, you're not just a reader; you're a trailblazer, helping to keep the flame of financial education burning bright. Let's keep this game going, one review at a time!

With gratitude,

Freddie Grant

CONCLUSION

Now that we're at the end let's take some time to reflect on the journey we've undertaken together. This book was not just about understanding money. Sure, you might have gained a few important insights and lessons along the way. But more than just developing your understanding, this book was designed to empower you. You are a member of this world's future generation. You should be armed with the knowledge to make informed financial decisions that can better your own life and the lives of those around you.

In this book, we learned the essentials of budgeting, saving, investing, and planning for both the short and long term. We've covered how to responsibly use credit cards, manage debt and the importance of starting early when it comes to saving for retirement. Each chapter aims to equip you with the skills to navigate the financial challenges and opportunities you'll encounter.

Ultimately, it's not just about accumulating money and getting rich. Yes, that's a part of it. But don't lose sight of the bigger picture. Financial independence is about making informed choices, achieving stability, and opening doors to your dreams. This book has provided you with the keys to your financial destiny, and it's time to put them to use. And remember, your journey to financial independence doesn't end with the closing of this book. This is just the start of your journey, and there's a long road ahead. You have plenty of time to build on this foundational knowledge and create a life worth being proud of. Let your money work for you, and start building the empowered financial future you deserve.

If you feel like this book has given you the adequate tools and confidence to start that journey, please consider leaving a review. Share how this guide has helped you or can help others like you. Your feedback is not just appreciated; it's a catalyst for shared learning and growth.

BONUS CHAPTER

MONEY MANTRAS

To help shift your mindset toward a more positive and growth-oriented relationship with money, incorporating daily affirmations or "money mantras" can be incredibly powerful. These mantras are designed to reinforce a healthy, proactive, and positive perspective on finances. Here are 15 money mantras you can recite daily to foster a growth money mindset:

- "I am in control of my financial future."
- "Every day, I make smart choices that lead to financial success."
- "I am deserving of a prosperous and abundant life."
- "Wealth flows to me in expected and unexpected ways."
- "I am confident in my ability to manage my finances effectively."
- "Saving money comes naturally to me and brings me closer to my goals."
- "I am open to new opportunities for increasing my wealth."
- "My actions create constant prosperity."
- "I am learning to make my money work for me."
- "I am capable of overcoming any financial obstacles that come my way."
- "I am deserving of financial security and freedom."

- "Investing in my future is a priority for me."
- "I am transforming into someone who is wise with money."
- "My positive attitude toward money attracts financial opportunities."
- "Each dollar I save is a seed for my future financial success."

Reciting these mantras daily can help instill a positive and proactive approach to your finances. They serve as reminders of your capabilities, goals, and the positive relationship you are building with money. Over time, these affirmations can shift your mindset, influencing your financial behaviors and decisions in a constructive way.

101 TEEN SIDE HUSTLES

These side hustles can help you explore your interests, develop new skills, and earn extra income. Remember, it's important to check local laws and regulations regarding work permits and age restrictions for certain types of jobs.

1. Babysitting
2. Lawn mowing
3. Dog walking
4. Pet sitting
5. Car washing
6. Tutoring in a subject you excel at
7. Selling handmade crafts
8. House sitting
9. Selling baked goods
10. Computer repair services
11. Creating and managing social media content
12. Graphic design services
13. Web development
14. Selling photography
15. YouTube content creation
16. Streaming on platforms like Twitch
17. Creating and selling digital art
18. Teaching music lessons
19. Running errands for neighbors

20. Pool cleaning
21. Snow shoveling
22. Leaf raking
23. Garage sale organizing
24. Bookkeeping for small businesses
25. Freelance writing
26. Transcription services
27. Language translation
28. Voice-over work
29. Podcast editing
30. Online tutoring
31. Virtual assistant services
32. Social media marketing
33. SEO services
34. App development
35. Creating educational videos or courses
36. Personal shopping
37. Grocery delivery
38. Meal preparation services
39. Fitness training or coaching
40. Sports coaching
41. Dance instructing
42. Yoga instructing
43. Makeup or beauty services
44. Nail art services
45. Jewelry making and selling
46. Fashion design and tailoring
47. Bicycle repair and maintenance
48. Electronics recycling and refurbishing
49. Creating mobile phone apps
50. Custom T-shirt printing
51. Event planning assistance
52. DJ services for local events
53. Performing at events (music, magic, etc.)
54. Stand-up comedy
55. Acting in local theater or productions
56. Modeling for local boutiques or artists
57. Interior decorating advice

58. Gardening services
59. Selling plants or produce
60. Creating and selling zines or comics
61. Providing tech support
62. Game development
63. Creating and selling printables
64. Online surveys and market research participation
65. Mystery shopping
66. Participating in focus groups
67. Reviewing products and services
68. Brand ambassador roles
69. Street performance (music, art)
70. Custom skateboard or bicycle painting
71. Drone photography and videography
72. Virtual event organizing
73. Online course creation
74. Creating and selling e-books
75. Personalized gift-making (e.g., mugs, T-shirts)
76. Home organization services
77. Custom cake baking and decorating
78. Antique restoration
79. Collectible trading (cards, toys)
80. Flip items from garage sales or thrift stores
81. Creating and selling candles
82. Soap making and selling
83. Creating and selling bath bombs
84. Knitting or crochet, selling the products
85. Custom embroidery services
86. Pottery making and selling
87. Woodworking and selling small crafts
88. Metalworking or jewelry making
89. Upcycling furniture and selling it
90. Creating and selling handmade stationery
91. Making and selling seasonal decorations
92. Producing and selling music beats
93. Sound design for small projects
94. Online fitness or wellness coaching
95. Creating and managing fantasy sports teams

96. Teaching a foreign language
97. Hosting gaming tournaments
98. Organizing and leading local tours
99. Teaching computer skills to seniors
100. Running a community newsletter or blog
101. Creating and selling custom phone cases

BIBLIOGRAPHY

Aebischer, C. (2021, April 7). *28 business ideas for teens*. NerdWallet. https://www.nerd-wallet.com/article/small-business/business-ideas-for-teens

Aoki, K. (2023, August 24). *Online banks vs. traditional banks: Which are better?* Www.forbes.com. https://www.forbes.com/advisor/banking/online-banks-vs-traditional-banks/

Backman, M. (2017, July 23). *7 stats that show how today's teens are making smart money choices*. The Motley Fool. https://www.fool.com/retirement/2017/07/23/7-stats-that-show-how-todays-teens-are-making-smar.aspx

Baluch, A. (2022, July 14). *How to save money as a teenager*. The Balance. https://www.the-balancemoney.com/how-to-save-money-as-a-teenager-5204306

Bell, A. (2023, May 15). *What are the 5 purposes of budgeting?* Investopedia. https://www.investopedia.com/financial-edge/1109/6-reasons-why-you-need-a-budget.aspx

Blanco, L. (2020, February 1). *5 key budgeting basics for teens*. TODAY.com. https://www.today.com/parenting-guides/five-key-budgeting-basics-t177200

Bromberg, M. (2023, March 10). Investing for teens: What they should know. *Investopedia*. https://www.investopedia.com/investing-for-teens-7111843

Bundrick, H. (2022, January 18). *11 best personal expense tracker apps for 2022*. NerdWallet. https://www.nerdwallet.com/article/finance/expense-tracker-apps

Caldwell, M. (2022, January 14). *6 things you can do to reach your savings goals*. The Balance. https://www.thebalancemoney.com/how-to-set-and-reach-savings-goals-2386115

Cooper, T. (2022, June 9). *How to pay for college without student loans*. Www.bestcolleges.com. https://www.bestcolleges.com/resources/pay-for-college-without-student-loans/

18 types of bank services. (2017, January 27). IEduNote.com. https://www.iedunote.com/bank-services

Ellis, K. (2023, August 28). *The best way to start saving for college*. Ramsey Solutions. https://www.ramseysolutions.com/saving/saving-for-college-is-easier-than-you-think

Eneriz, A. (2022, April 13). *Debt avalanche vs. debt snowball: What's the difference?* Investopedia. https://www.investopedia.com/articles/personal-finance/080716/debt-avalanche-vs-debt-snowball-which-best-you.asp

Fernando, J. (2023, May 18). *Compound interest definition*. Investopedia. https://www.investopedia.com/terms/c/compoundinterest.asp

5 ways a growth mindset can achieve financial success. (n.d.). Investing Buff. Retrieved January 6, 2024, from https://investingbuff.com/mindset-shifts-for-financial-wellness/emotional-intelligence/growth-mindset/

Glazer, J. (2023, May 20). *Teen summer job seekers: Unlock your path to success with these pointers. this one is for you!* Www.linkedin.com. https://www.linkedin.com/pulse/teen-summer-job-seekers-unlock-your-path-success-pointers-glazer/

Goldberg, M. (2022, June 30). *Savings strategies for different goals*. Bankrate.

https://www.bankrate.com/banking/savings/savings-strategies-for-different-goals/

Gravier, E. (2023, June 14). *1.6% of Americans have a perfect 850 credit score, but here's the only one that matters, according to experts.* CNBC. https://www.cnbc.com/select/what-credit-score-should-you-have/

How to make a zero-based budget. (2024, January 3). Ramsey Solutions. https://www.ramseysolutions.com/budgeting/how-to-make-a-zero-based-budget

Issa, E. E., & O'Shea, B. (2023, December 18). *How to build credit.* NerdWallet. https://www.nerdwallet.com/article/finance/how-to-build-credit

Jespersen, C. (2020, December 15). *5 steps for tracking your monthly expenses.* NerdWallet. https://www.nerdwallet.com/article/finance/tracking-monthly-expenses

Kenner, J. (n.d.). *4 benefits of starting a business as a teenager.* Www.leangap.org. https://www.leangap.org/articles/4-benefits-of-starting-a-business-as-a-teenager

Kenton, W. (2022, February 9). *What is personal finance, and why is it important?* Investopedia. https://www.investopedia.com/terms/p/personalfinance.asp

Kissinger, M. (2019, March 9). *Reasons why the 9-5 job no longer makes financial sense.* Www.linkedin.com. https://www.linkedin.com/pulse/cheating-from-womans-mans-point-michael-kissinger/

Kurt, D. (2019). *Emergency funds and new ways to get one.* Investopedia. https://www.investopedia.com/terms/e/emergency_fund.asp

Lambarena, M., & Tierney, S. (2021, November 24). *How to choose a bank.* NerdWallet. https://www.nerdwallet.com/article/banking/how-to-choose-a-bank

Money mindsets: How to change your financial mindset. (2023, April 12). Loqbox. https://www.loqbox.com/en-gb/blog/money-mindsets-how-to-change-your-financial-mindset

Picardo, E. (2022, July 22). *Investing explained: Types of investments and how to get started.* Investopedia. https://www.investopedia.com/terms/i/investing.asp

Polglase, A. (2023, March 8). *How to set up a budget and stick to it.* Hyperjar. https://hyperjar.com/blog/how-to-stick-to-a-budget

Pyles, S. (2023, February 21). *Good debt vs. bad debt: Examples and solutions.* NerdWallet. https://www.nerdwallet.com/article/finance/good-debt-vs-bad-debt

Rowan, E. (2023, April 13). *5 smart shopping habits that help you spend less and live better.* Andrew Rowan Wealth Management. https://www.arwm.com.au/5-smart-shopping-habits-that-help-you-spend-less-and-live-better/

Segal, T. (2023, July 1). *The ins and outs of diversification.* Investopedia. https://www.investopedia.com/terms/d/diversification.asp

Smith, L. (2020, January 31). *The true cost of owning a car.* Investopedia. https://www.investopedia.com/articles/pf/08/cost-car-ownership.asp

Tarpley, L. G., & Acevedo, S. (2023, November 15). *6 types of savings accounts.* Business Insider. https://www.businessinsider.com/personal-finance/types-of-savings-accounts?r=US&IR=T

10 strategies to avoid getting into debt. (n.d.). Central Bank. https://www.central-bank.net/learning-center/strategies-to-avoid-debt/

Top 7 important personal finance skills. (2020, May 21). The Corporate Investor. https://thecorporateinvestor.net/important-personal-finance-skills/

Trumbower, D. (2023, July 27). *How to help your teenage child become a Roth IRA millionaire.* Retirement Daily on TheStreet: Finance and Retirement Advice, Analysis, and More. https://www.thestreet.com/retirement-daily/your-money/how-to-help-your-teenage-child-become-a-roth-ira-millionaire

Ulzheimer, J. (2023, July 31). *How many Americans have bad credit? (2024).* Bad Credit. https://www.badcredit.org/how-to/how-many-americans-have-bad-credit/

Vandiver, W., & Bradley, S. (2023, November 30). *What is the total cost of owning a car?* NerdWallet. https://www.nerdwallet.com/article/loans/auto-loans/total-cost-owning-car

Waugh, E. (2023, February 11). *How to stop impulse spending.* Experian. https://www.experian.com/blogs/ask-experian/how-to-stop-impulse-spending/

Weston, L. (2022, September 23). *Why your credit score is important.* NerdWallet. https://www.nerdwallet.com/article/finance/great-credit-powerful-tool

Zdunek, J. (2015, December 4). *How to balance school and a part-time job.* TeenLife. https://www.teenlife.com/blog/how-balance-school-and-part-time-job/